The Dissertation and Research Cookbook From Soup to Nuts

A Practical Guide to Help You Start and Complete Your Dissertation or Research Project

Third Edition

Marilyn K. Simon, Ph.D.
J. Bruce Francis, Ph.D.

Cover images © 2001 PhotoDisc, Inc.

Changes in the Third Edition

The third edition of *The Dissertation and Research Cookbook* includes many familiar and new features intended to guide you through the research process in a positive and supportive way, and to assuage any concerns you might have about any aspect of doing quality contributory research.

In response to extensive surveys, focus groups, and in-depth reviewer feedback, every phase of *The Dissertation and Research Cookbook* has been carefully revised and fully edited to ensure appropriate content coverage and the highest degree of accuracy.

Highlights of Content Changes:

1. URL's for websites have been added in most sections. This will be helpful in making sure that you have the latest information you need to do research today. However, since websites are living documents, they do *change* and some might not be available when you check for them, and better websites are yet to be written. We apologize in advance if you visit a website that is no longer active, or is busy when you try to click on.
2. More information on data analysis has been added. In particular, there is a great deal of information on non-parametric data analysis, which is common, and becoming more common, in many research projects for the social sciences.
3. More information on different research methodologies to help classify your research study.
4. An expanded bibliography has been added.

Research is a systematic, structured, purposeful, and disciplined process of discovery. Since each type of knowledge is unique, *The Dissertation and Research Cookbook* presents a variety of systematic methods to access different types of knowledge. If your research is carefully planned and conducted, and contains the appropriate ingredients, an analysis of data will produce valuable descriptions and inferences about the phenomenon you are investigating. Following the recommended "recipes" will enable you to "relish" the entire process.

The Dissertation and Research Cookbook will guide you through the preliminary preparation of your research, the research process itself, and assist you in reporting your findings so that others can benefit from the "fruits" of your labor. In this way you will be able to make valuable contributions to the knowledge base of your field of study. Enjoy the preparation and the feast!

Contents

Phase 3—The Feast [Your Dissertation/Research Paper]

Phase 1
Planning Your Feast: Getting Started

Proceed [7 Easy Steps to a Great Start]

Pick Your Repast [Choose Your Topic]

Classify Your Repast—"What's Cooking?" [Identify Your Study]

Be Aware of Health Hazards [Ethics of Research]

Choose Your Attire [Form and Style]

Putting together an excellent dissertation, or formal research project, is like planning and preparing a gourmet feast for a gathering of distinguished guests. You, the researcher, can think of yourself as the chef and chief meal engineer for this eloquent repast.

Congratulations! By procuring your copy of *The Dissertation and Research Cookbook,* and reading the information provided here, you have taken an important first step to secure the successful realization of your goal—you have shown an interest. Your next step is to turn your interest into result-getting actions.

The following ingredients are part of your *The Dissertation and Research Cookbook*'s recipe for an excellent "feast" (dissertation/research paper). An acronym, decree, and seven-step recipe that will insure your initial and ultimate success is:

Proceed!

1 c.   "P"ossess a Positive Attitude

1 c.   "R"ead Efficiently—Understand Scholarly Language

1 c.   "O"rganize Your Time

1 c.   "C"reate a Working Environment

1 c.   "E"xtend Your Note Taking and Writing Skills—Record Keeping, Mind Mapping, and PIE Writing

1 c.   "E"nter Information into a Computer, Journal, or Tape Deck

1 c.   "D"esign a Survival Kit

1 c. "P"ossess a Positive Attitude

For a positive attitude, mix a dash of each: visualization, exercise, determination, and sound nutrition. Remember: Your attitudes shape your future!

If your formal research project is for professional advancement, it is important that you choose a project that you, your advisors, mentors, and sponsors are enthusiastic about. Arnold Schwarzenegger, five-time Mr. Universe and four-time Mr. Olympic, told reporters, "As long as your mind can envision that you can do something, then you can do it."

The following activities will enable you to use visualization techniques to assist you in creating and maintaining a positive attitude through the successful completion of your dissertation or research project.

1. Visualize yourself successfully producing an excellent dissertation or research project.
2. Imagine enjoying each aspect of creating your dissertation or research project.
3. Conjure up an image of yourself working in a pleasant environment, accomplishing the goals that you will recognize and see to fruition.
4. Picture yourself obtaining the degree and/or recognition you are seeking.
5. Repeat these steps each time you begin work on your dissertation/research project.

Fill out the information on the cutting board to further assist you in visualizing your preparation of an outstanding "feast."

Cutting Board:

1. Take a few minutes to reflect upon the benefits you will receive upon the successful completion of your goal. What are some of those benefits? _____
   _____
2. If you are planning to do a dissertation, take a look at the table of contents Phase 3—The Feast [Your Dissertation]. These are the ingredients (Chapters) that constitute most dissertations. Take a moment to digest this information.
   Imagine what your dissertation will look like. Can you see it bound with your name and degree on the cover? _____ Will you have it hardbound or soft bound or both? _____ How many copies do you think you will make of your final dissertation text? _____
3. Most dissertations are between 100 and 200 pages, while research papers can be significantly less. Approximately how many pages do you envision your dissertation or research paper to be? _____
4. Do you envision having graphs and charts? _____ How many references do you think you will have consulted? _____
5. What will change once you get your degree or finish your research?
6. Who will you tell about your successes?
7. What do you see as their reaction?
8. What type of support system do you have or need to obtain?
9. If you are hoping to obtain a Ph.D., then the next time you call directory assistance introduce yourself as Dr. (surname), and see how that title feels to you.

Your body and mind are closely related. Your mental efficiency is affected by the state of your body. Check to see that your diet is healthful. Many studies suggest that protein helps keep the brain alert and that the brain's performance is also affected by choline (a B-complex vitamin that is found in egg yolks, beef liver, fish, raisins, and legumes). Other B vitamins as well as Vitamin C and iron are also essential in maintaining a healthy brain.

Stay away from alcohol during your dissertation working days. See to it that your exercise is efficient and enjoyable. At the very minimum you should be doing 20 minutes of cardiovascular exercise three times a week. Thirty minutes a day of a fitness program that combines flexibility, endurance, and strength is better. The mental effects of regular exercise are profound and extensive, touching your intellect, memory, and emotions.

Cutting Board:

1. What in your diet needs to be improved so that you have the best possible nutrition?
   _____

2. What type of exercise do you enjoy doing that could help you become more fit?
   _____

3. What other measures can you take to support yourself in obtaining your goal?
   _____

4. Sleep is important for the renewed health of the brain. When you drift off into dreamland—a procedure that happens in stages—your brain goes through a series of psychological processes that restores both mind and body. At certain stages memories are consolidated and at other stages your brain is working out resolutions to unconscious conflicts. The use of alcohol or drugs, a noisy bedroom, an uncomfortable bed, stress carried over from the day, or other disruptions may upset this pattern.

   Too much sleep can be as detrimental as too little sleep. Most adults do very well with 6-8 hours of sleep.

   How much sleep do you really need to feel great? _____ See that you get that amount during your research working days and try to eliminate any conditions that disrupt your sleep.

---

1 c. "R"ead Efficiently—Understand Scholarly Language

The book exists for us perchance which will explain our miracles and reveal new ones.

Walden—Henry David Thoreau

All research projects, and thus dissertations, require a voluminous amount of reading from texts, journals, periodicals, newspapers, web pages, etc. The following tasks have been employed by successful researchers to help make their reading more productive. Put an asterisk (*) next to the activities that you already cultivate, and an exclamation mark (!) next to the ones that you could employ to make your reading more constructive. You will find more "helpful hints" in the Literature Review Section of Phase 3. If you have already mastered the information below, perhaps you should check out that section now.

_____1. Take time to reflect on what it is you are hoping to find before you begin to read.

_____2. Survey the table of contents and note major headings.

_____3.	If there are chapter summaries in a text, or an abstract for a paper, read them before exploring the chapter or paper.

_____4.	As you read, try to relate the information to something you are already familiar with.

_____5.	Take notes or highlight important ideas. If you can do this at the keyboard you can save yourself quite a bit of time.

_____6.	Check for patterns the author might be applying, such as:

Cause and Effect: The author explains a situation or theory and then delves into the consequences of its application.

Compare/Contrast: The author examines two or more different theories or situations and their relationship to each other.

Process-Description: A certain concept, program, or project is delineated and then examples are provided.

Sequential: A case is built in a linear or historical manner.

_____7.	Be an active reader. Always ask yourself questions about what you are reading, such as: What is the author's purpose? Why am I reading this? What conclusions does the author come to? Is this reasonable? Who else supports this view?

_____8.	Imagine that the author is personally speaking with you (just like your *Dissertation Cookbook* does).

Check out: *http://www.umi.com/hp/Support/DServices/* to find out how to find dissertations in your field.

Academic Writing

In academic writing, a specialized form of discourse often develops. At times this rarefied language is necessary to capture the complexity and distinctiveness of processes that cannot easily be described in colloquial terms. At other times, however, writers throw around terms that are understood only by an "in" group of ideologically sympathetic theorists.

Words are weapons; they have great power invested in them. They create, as well as mirror, reality. They serve to advance certain ideals, images, stereotypes, paradigms, and sets of assumptions. They play an important role in creating the conditions for educational discourse. They frame what are considered to be the limits of acceptable practices, philosophies, and purposes, and they are governed by logic at the most abstract level of critical analysis.

When you write in an academic manner, you are identified as a "member of the club of scholars." Those who "consume" what you write can substantiate it. Academic writing enables academicians to express ideas more forcefully and intelligently, and helps eliminate ambiguity. A negative effect is that it can also be used (intentionally or unintentionally) to intimidate those "not in the club." Scholarly literacy is a moving target, and it is thus crucial that you keep up with the professional literature to be aware of the terminology in current use.

In order to cope with the demands of a discipline, you must be able to grasp the implications of important concepts that permeate the literature. For example, in reading scholarly work you will frequently come across such terms as: paradigm, theory, validity, bias, etc. It is important to understand the meaning of these terms in the context in which they are found. Many of these important terms can be found in various sections of your *Dissertation Cookbook*.

Some Scholarly Jargon

Ontological: What is the nature of the "knowable," or of "reality"? How is the social world perceived and understood? (Hitchcock & Hughes, 1995)

Epistemological: What is the nature of the relationship between the knower (the inquirer) and the known (or knowable)? A theory of knowing and the nature of knowing; ways to justify beliefs (Hitchcock & Hughes, 1995).

Conceptual or Theoretical Framework: What are potential explanations or potential relationships for a situation or problem? A theoretical framework helps to place a study in perspective among other studies and to justify asking the subjects to take part. It is used to support studies looking for relationships between variables. For example, a relationship might exist between prenatal nutrition of mothers and intellectual performance of their offspring. As Wood and Brink (1989) pointed out, "If no conceptual framework is provided, there is no indication of where the study might fit in the universe of research and thus the value of the study is questionable" (pp. 108-109). The Diffusion of Innovation framework states that adopting innovation is a process that includes the following steps: knowledge, attitude, decision implementation, and confirmation. This framework characterizes individuals through the use of five categories: innovators, early adopters, early majority, late majority, and laggards. How the investigator views the world affects the entire process—from conceptualizing a problem, to collecting and analyzing data, to interpreting the findings.

If a conceptual framework has not already been developed, an exploratory study might be appropriate. Using our example above, if there had been no testing of the notion that there is a relationship between prenatal nutrition and the intellectual ability of the child, an exploratory study would be required. The conceptual framework is usually summarized in the form of questions supporting the tentative nature of the framework. That is, no unwarranted emphasis is placed on the thoughts about the relationship.

Theory: Webster's New Dictionary (2000) defines a theory as "A set of interconnected statements that integrate information within a field of inquiry and suggest a new relationship among the phenomena under study. " Theories serve several purposes—primarily descriptive. They describe the nature and conditions in which human behavior operates. They also set limits or boundaries for which the theorist is responsible. Another function is to generate new ideas for research by suggesting specific relationships that will need further study. Theories also attempt to bring together ideas, facts, observations, and other theories into systems of thought or meaning (Salkind, 1985, p. 6). The extent to which observations can be accounted for by a theory is the extent to which a theory is credible.

Methodology: How should the inquirer go about finding out knowledge? A broad, complex array of ideas, concepts, frameworks, and theories surround the use of various methods or techniques employed to generate data on the social world. Questions about the collection of quantitative data via surveys or questionnaires, or qualitative data via participation and involvement, for example, are methodological questions.

Variable: A factor, phenomenon, or characteristic that has more than one value or category either quantitative or qualitative. If only one value is possible it is a constant and not a variable (Sproull, 1995). A dependent variable (y-value) depends on some other variable, which has usually preceded it in time. An independent variable (x-value) can be manipulated, measured, or selected prior to measuring the outcome or dependent variable.

Existentialism: A term that designates a concern in philosophy, literature, and art with the irreducibly personal and subjective aspects of human existence. Soren Kierkegaard and Friedrich Nietzsche are often considered the "fathers" of existentialism. Other prominent names associated with existentialism are Fyodor Dostoevsky, Martin Heidegger, Jean-Paul Sartre, Albert Camus, and Simone de Beauvoir (who might be called the "mother" of feminist existentialism and of feminism at large). Contemporary expressions of existentialism can be found in the novels of Milan Kundera (e.g., *The Unbearable Lightness of Being*), some of the films of Woody Allen (e.g., *Crimes and Misdemeanors*), and Peter Shaffer's play *Equus*. Some themes found in existentialism include an emphasis upon the individual, a critique of current society, the goal of a comfortable existence, objectivity, and an emphasis upon the dynamic and incomplete versus the static and complete.

Constructivism: A theoretical framework that has its roots in medieval philosophy and has been applied to sociology and anthropology, as well as cognitive psychology and education. The constructivist philosopher Giambatista Vico commented in a treatise in 1710 that "one only knows something if one can explain it " (Yager, 1991). Immanual Kant further elaborated this idea by asserting that human beings are not passive recipients of information. Learners actively take knowledge, connect it to previously assimilated knowledge and make it theirs by constructing their own interpretation (Cheek, 1992). In a constructivist setting, knowledge is not objective; meaning is intimately connected with experience.

Postmodernism: Postmodernism and Critical Theory are broad rubrics for intellectual movements rather than specific theories. Perhaps the most characteristic tenet of postmodern critical work is that what European philosophy and science has held to be fundamentally true at an abstract level (ontology, epistemology, metaphysics, logic) is in fact a contingent, historically specific cultural construction, which has often served the function of empowering members of a dominant social class at the expense of others. The postmodern movement dismantles foundational procedures and assumptions whereby to establish universal truths or principles. It is fundamentally a revolutionary political movement, argued in intellectual terms. For more information see *http://www.cs.cmu.edu/afs/ cs.cmu.edu/user/phoebe/mosaic/postmodernism.html*

The following adages illustrate both the beauty and the bafflement one encounters in scholarly discourse. These two "simple statements" epitomize how brevity can belie the complexity inherent in the language of the scholar. Determine which "camp" you are in, or under which conditions you favor one philosophy over the other. Try saying and sharing these expressions with a friend or colleague. This will make you sound like a true scholar.

Camp 1: Epistemology Presupposes Ontology—This is the realist view, which contends that in order to know (episteme) there must be something real (ontos) to know. It is a belief favored by those who employ quantitative methodologies. Members of this camp contend there is a "solution" to a problem that can be found using the scientific method of deduction.

Camp 2: Ontology Presupposes Epistemology—This is the constructivist view, which contends that our knowing (episteme) gives reality its realness (ontos). It is a belief held by postmodernist and constructivists who believe that there is no one reality and that context is everything. Qualitative methodologists support this notion with the belief that reality is socially constructed through individual or collective definitions of the situation. This philosophy is more concerned with understanding and consistency than with trying to explain a phenomenon. Members of the constructivist camp contend that conclusions are based on induction and context sensitivity, and that universal, context-free generalizations do not exist.

Cutting Board:

1. Which of the active reading strategies above do you already employ? _____
2. Which of these suggestions do you need to practice?_____
3. Which of the two "camps" are you a member of? _____ Why?
   _____

1 c. "O"rganize Your Time

By planning your future, you can live in the present . . . Time is one of your most valuable resources, and it is important that you spend it wisely.

Lee Berglund—founder of Personal Resource Systems

The key point in time management is recognizing the finite nature of time as a resource. This is both good news and bad news. The bad news, of course, is that time is limited. It moves at the same rate and there is no way to manipulate the passage of time. The good news is that time is a constant. It is known and, hence, its stability provides a basis for predicting future outcomes.

Time management includes good program planning whereby resources (people, time) can be used effectively. Daily work is made easier when a model provides a continuing guide for action and various levels of accountability and responsibility. Such a model also specifies essential tasks and sequences of tasks along with a timeline for completion.

Managing time is a decision process. It is a set of decisions that parse time as a finite resource among tasks that are competing for this resource. The effectiveness of such decisions is an outcome of task achievement skills as well as the priority assigned to each task. The quality and quantity of any outcome is dependent on the skill with which the task was addressed and the amount of time that was devoted to the task.

An excellent first step in effective time and activity management is to write down your goals. On the cutting board below write down the day that you plan to complete your dissertation (or research project), "DCD" or "RCD." (You might want to do this after you have completed Phase 1 of your *Dissertation Cookbook*.)

My DCD/RCD will be _____(date). At that time I will have successfully completed the written part of my dissertation/research project and sent it to the proper authorities.

Next, it is important that you recognize other things that you have to do and want to do between now and DCD or RCD.

On the cutting board below write down the things in your life that you have to do and then the things that are not on the list that you want to do between now and DCD or RCD.

___

Cutting Board:

1. I have to do the following activities between now and DCD or RCD: _____

2. In addition I want to do the following activities: _____

___

Good Job! Now let us break this down into smaller chunks and make a plan for next week. First, fill in the following calendar with all the time that you will be attending to your "have to's." Next, fill in quality time that you can dedicate to your research. Choose something that you want to do that is not on the schedule, and plan for that as well.

Monday	Tuesday	Wednesday	Thursday	Friday	Saturday	Sunday

Cutting Board:

1. Make an affirmation for the next 7 days.
       By _____I will have achieved the following goals in my research:
    _____

2. Make an affirmation for the next month.
       By _____I will have achieved the following goals in my research:
    _____

- Begin each new week with a similar affirmation until DCD or RCD.
- Remember to achieve a goal it must be: Conceivable—capable of being put into words; Believable—to you; Achievable—you have the strength, energy, and time to accomplish it.

There are many activities that you can do to support yourself in the preparation and serving of your feast. You may want to learn how to use the computer in a university library, learn a new software program such as EXCEL or SPSS, familiarize yourself with APA formatting (*http://www.perrla.com*), learn how to do on-line searches on the Internet, *http://www.kryltech.com* or purchase a new or used computer. Software companies like Guildford *http://www.guilford.com* provide programs to assist you with some research tasks. You also may need to obtain office supplies, research a variety of preliminary topics, take a refresher course in statistics at a local college, consult with advisors in your field or in other fields, relieve yourself from prior responsibilities, etc.

On the cutting board below, make a list of five things that will support you in completing your research by DCD or RCD, and times that you will be able to attend to these things.

Cutting Board:

By _____(date) I will :_____

By _____(date) I will :_____

By _____(date) I will :_____

By _____(date) I will :_____

By _____(date) I will :_____

Some additional time management tips:

1. Learn to Prioritize. Prioritizing your responsibilities and engagements is very important. One method is the DWM list. This list is divided into three sections, obviously enough, D, W, and M. The items placed in the D section are those needed to be done that day. The items placed in the W section need completion within the week. The M section items are those things that need to be done within the month.
2. Combine several activities—multi-tasking. While commuting to work, listen to taped notes or books on tape. This allows up to an hour or two a day of good study review. While showering make a mental list of the things that need to be done. When you watch a sit-com, laugh as you pay your bills. These are just suggestions of what you can do to combine your time, but there are many others. Above all be creative, and let it work for you.
3. After scheduling becomes a habit, you can adjust the existing schedule. It's better to be precise at first. It is easier to find something to do with extra time than to find extra time to do something. Most importantly, make it work for you. A time schedule that is not personalized and honest is not a time schedule at all. Be flexible . . . life happens!
4. Don't be a perfectionist. Trying to be a perfect person sets you up for defeat. Nobody can be perfect. Difficult tasks usually result in avoidance and procrastination. You need to set achievable goals, but they should also be challenging. There will always be people both weaker and stronger than you.
5. Learn to say no. For example, an acquaintance of yours would like you to see a movie with him/her tonight. You made social plans for tomorrow with your friends and tonight you were going to read a journal article that you just received relating to your research. You really are not interested in this movie. You want to say no, but you hate turning people down. Politely saying no should become a habit. Saying no frees up time for the things that are most important.
6. Understand when you are most efficient. During the times when you feel the most alert you should be doing the most creative and original aspects of your research. When you are less alert you can still work on some of the more mundane tasks like formatting or doing searches.

1 c. "C"reating a Working Environment

Your own space—a little time with your own thoughts in (your) own space . . .
where there is no one else but (you) to meet inside. [A place which is relatively
serene and conducive for productive work. A place where you have the freedom
to think and work on your research]. "My Own Space"

(The Act)—a play by Fred Ebb

Your special space or your "kitchen" where you will be preparing your feast should have the following luxuries:

1. Proper lighting. Poor lighting increases eye fatigue. Ideal lighting is indirect and free from glare.
2. Proper ventilation. The brain needs fresh oxygen to function at its optimum.
3. Reasonable quietness. Try experimenting with soft classical or jazz music in the background, and see if that increases your concentration and productivity.
4. Proper supplies and support systems. (See Designing a Survival Kit.)
5. A DO NOT DISTURB sign. When you display this sign, it needs to be respected by those with whom you live.
6. Optional: There is a subtle but intimate connection between our olfactory environment and our mental and emotional well-being. The fragrance of vanilla can be very soothing, and peppermint can help improve task performance.

1 c. "E"xtend Your Note Taking and Writing Skills—Record Keeping, Mind Mapping, and PIE Writing

You might find it handy to use 3" x 5" index cards to keep a record of references (titles of books or periodicals), which you feel pertain to your research. (You should also periodically store them in a program on your computer.) You will want to be sure that you note the author's name, the reference—book, journal, magazine article—publisher, relevant page numbers, any excerpts you might want to cite, and the exact page numbers of potential quotations.

You might also consider using different colors to indicate different types of references; for example, pink cards could be used for texts, green for periodicals, yellow for research reports, etc. This system will be extremely helpful to you when preparing the Research/Literature Chapter of your dissertation (see Phase 3) or research project, and compiling your bibliography. You might also wish to create folders to store articles and references that you obtain related to your topic.

If you choose to use your laptop computer or PDA to take notes, you'll find excellent note-taking capabilities in the simple text editors that come bundled with most machines, and strong organizing capabilities in the database software that is easily available.

Note Taking

A new form of note taking that is rapidly replacing the traditional outline form of note taking is mind mapping. Some characteristics of a mind map are that it:

1. Stimulates the way that most people think.
2. Is a means of brainstorming that allows your thoughts to flow freely.
3. Helps you to categorize information and determine how this information relates to other information.
4. Gives you an overview of your project.

Figure 1 is a mind map of a mind map. Carefully study the mind map for its structure, purpose, and usefulness. Notice that a mind map requires only one page (preferably a blank page which is held horizontally) where related ideas are linked together. The Roman numerals that are used in traditional outlining appear as branches on a mind map.

Note: Researchers claim that people who have switched from traditional outlining to mind mapping significantly increase their retention and heighten their organizational skills. In addition, mind mapping is fun, easy, and creative. Try using colored pens or pencils when creating mind maps. Experiment with each branch illustrated in a different color. You might want different shades of a particular color to signify supporting ideas.

Mind Mapping

Tony Buzan of the Learning Methods Group in England originated mind mapping. This technique is based on research findings that show that the brain works primarily with key concepts in an interrelated and integrated manner. Traditional thinking opts for columns and rows as illustrated by traditional outlining techniques. Buzan felt that "working out" from a core idea would suit the brain's thinking patterns better. The brain also needs a way to "slot in" ideas that are relevant to the core idea. To achieve those ends, Buzan developed mind mapping.

Mind mapping is an individual brainstorming process. In brainstorming, you are interested in generating as many ideas as possible, even wild and crazy ones. Just write or otherwise record whatever comes into your head, as it occurs. Quantity, not quality, is what you are after. No criticism is allowed during the brainstorming itself. Later you can go back and critique your inputs or those of others. You can also generate new ideas by looking at what you have already written—"piggybacking" on the work you've done before.

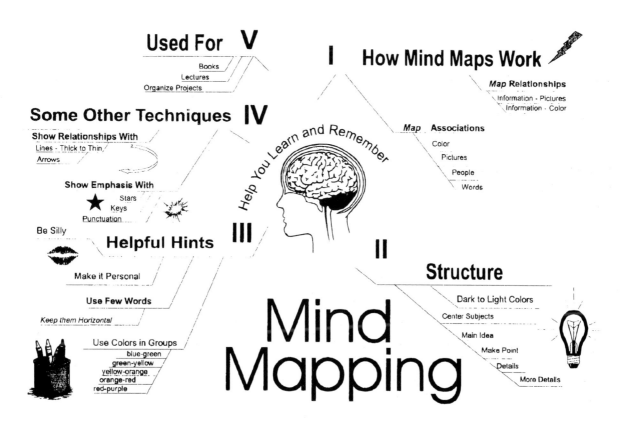

Figure 1 A mind map of mind mapping

To begin a mind-mapping session, write the name or a brief description of the object or problem in the center of a piece of paper and draw a circle around it. Then brainstorm each major facet of that object or problem, drawing lines outward from the circle like roads leaving a city. You can draw branches from those "roads" as you brainstorm them in more detail.

You can brainstorm all the main lines at once and then the branches for each. Or you can brainstorm a line and its branches before moving on to the next line. Or you can jump from place to place as thoughts occur. To make the mind map more useful, you might draw each major branch extending from your central thought in a different color. As you branch out, you may notice related topics appearing on different branches. You can emphasize those relationships by circling the items in question or by drawing lines under or between them.

Finally, study your mind map and look for interrelationships and terms that appear more than once. Mind mapping is an excellent technique, not only for generating new ideas, but also for developing one's intuitive capacity. It is especially useful for identifying all the issues and sub-issues related to a problem, as well as possible solutions to a problem. To do that, use the main branches on your mind map for solutions; the sub-branches from each of them become the perceived benefits and obstacles related to these solutions. Mind mapping also works well for outlining presentations, papers, and book chapters. In fact, it is useful in a wide variety of situations. For more information on mind mapping see *http://www.ozemail.com.au/~caveman/Creative/Mindmap/*.

Cutting Board:

Use a blank sheet of paper to create a mind map of a topic that you might want to research. Put the name of the topic in the middle of the paper. Use branches to indicate main ideas (beliefs, attitudes, and opinions) related to this topic. Several excellent computer programs are available for mind mapping, including Verio by Microsoft and Inspiration.

To transform your notes into written passages, you might want to try a formula developed by Hanau (1975). Hanau advanced the idea that written materials contain statements, which are the declaration of beliefs, attitudes, or opinions. These statements are the keys that allow the reader to understand what you, the writer, are trying to convey. Each paragraph should contain a statement or statements in conjunction with supporting elements that have the function of elucidating the statement. These supporting elements can be classified into one of the three categories, which can be remembered by the acronym PIE: Proof, Information, or Examples.

1. Proof—any kind of supporting documentation that a statement is true and/or important. In a dissertation or research paper, proof usually comes from a review of related research or a quote from a well-known person, authority figure, or document.
2. Information—any clarifying material, such as a definition, which limits the scope of your statements and seeks to make clear what your statements mean within a certain context. This clarification brings your supporting material to bear in an effective manner.
3. Example—a concrete illustration that serves to clarify any statement that you make while attesting to a statement's truth or importance.

It is not necessary to have all three supporting elements in every paragraph of your paper, but you will probably wish to include at least two "pieces of PIE" per paragraph. You also need not adhere to any particular order of presenting a "statement" with its accompanying pieces of PIE, so long as your paragraphs are clear, sufficiently detailed, and coherent.

On the other hand, if your paragraphs are only statements without any pieces of PIE, the predominant impression that comes across is assertion without foundation. Similarly, having pieces of PIE without a statement makes it difficult for the reader to comprehend the point of what is written. Once your paragraph has a statement with a satisfactory helping of PIE, you are ready to move to the next paragraph.

Cutting Board:

Look at the main branches of the mind map that you created on a topic that you might wish to research. See if you can support these ideas (main branches) with the PIE elements described in this section.

---

1 c. "E"nter Information into a Computer, Tape Deck, or Journal

Alfieri, the great Italian dramatist, allegedly had his servants tie him to his writing table so that he would be forced to write.

Hopefully, you will not need to go to the extremes that Alfieri did to discipline yourself into putting your thoughts and notes into the formation of your "feast."

Much of what makes writing difficult is trying to write and edit at the same time. Get your ideas on paper first; critique, rework, and polish them later. Critiquing ideas as you are trying to express them often represses them. If you reach a stumbling block, try to write past it—often the best ideas lie right beyond the hurdle tempting you to give up. If you are still stuck, take a break and think over the problem in a relaxed setting. By the time you return, you will probably have the answer.

Be prepared to write at any time, in any place. Keep pen and paper in your car, purse, gym bag, pocket, etc., or keep your PDA handy and/or your laptop in standby mode. The best ideas often come when you are not trying for them. If you are adept at word processing, you can save yourself a significant amount of time by regularly transposing your notes into your computer.

If you are fortunate enough to have a dedicated secretary and he/she is used to transcribing your dictation into a word processor, that might be your ideal method for formulating your dissertation. This method of transcription offers you the liberty of creating your "feast" while in the midst of traffic. You can experiment with tape recording your ideas and using voice dictation software like Dragon Naturally Speaking to transcribe your notes. Voice-activated word processing programs are getting better each day.

If computers are not your "thing," and you do not have a secretary to transcribe your notes, perhaps you and your feast would be best served by obtaining a wonderful pen and an ingratiating journal and proceeding to WRITE. When your document is near completion, you should probably hire someone to enter it into a word processor so that you can make corrections and deletions and obtain an exquisite feast shortly thereafter. Be aware, however, that mastering the computer will have many benefits now (faster completion of work) and later (most organizations require a high degree of computer literacy).

Cutting Board:

1. What will you use to create your feast? _____
2. When will be your first (next) time to use this method? _____

The following is a rubric that can be used to help develop better writing skills. You might want to write a few pages and then ask someone whose opinion you value to critique what you have written based on this rubric.

Rubric for Writing	0	1	2	3
General Organization: coherency/integration				
Each paragraph is fully developed and related to the question or intent of the paper.				
Each paragraph begins with a topic sentence that introduces and summarizes the point to be made.				
There is clarity of thought and expression. The author's meaning is always clear.				
The reader can follow the author's thoughts easily throughout the essay.				
Words are well chosen; statements are free from contradiction, the essay as a whole is free of jargon and clichés.				
The writing is free from grammatical, punctuation, and spelling errors.				
There is a clear statement of thesis in the writing; in it the author defines the boundaries of the document.				
Wholeness: The author presents the topics to be addressed in an integrated way and summarizes the major points.				
The writing has cadence and flows easily; the reader can sense the person behind the words.				

0 = Blank, off topic, incoherent.
1 = Below average, weak subject knowledge.
2 = Satisfactory, average, demonstrates a basic understanding of the information.
3 = Above average, outstanding. Demonstrates a thorough understanding of the issue. Provides a strong explanation and understanding of the concepts and information relevant to the subject and issues.

Creating a Journal

Journals and diaries have a long history as a means of self-expression. By keeping a learning journal you can write away . . . Stress, Anxiety, Indecision, Problems, Unfinished Business, Confusion, Writer's Block, and Procrastination

There are many benefits to be gained by keeping a journal. Some benefits of keeping a journal include:

1. Writing can flow without self-consciousness or inhibition.
2. Your thought processes and mental habits can be revealed.
3. You can improve your memory.
4. You can provide tangible evidence of mental processes.
5. You can obtain mental growth through critical reflection.
6. You can help make meaning out of what is experienced or read as it relates to your research.
7. You can articulate connections between new information and what you know.

One type of journal you might wish to keep is known as a reader response journal or literature log. Here you can record the response to your readings. It enables you to enter the literature in your "own voice." If you would like to keep your personal diary or journal online, Cam Development at *http://www.camdevelopment.com/mpd.htm* has some excellent software to assist you.

1 c. "D"esign a Survival Kit

The following is a list of supplies and tools that you might find helpful to have in your "kitchen" while designing your "feast."

Computer	Modem	Printer
Pencils	Pencil sharpener	Erasers
Ruler	Graph paper	Wastebasket
Dictionary	Thesaurus	Encyclopedia
Scissors	Three hole punch	Tape
Bookcase	Writing table	Computer paper
Highlighters	Colored pens	Paper clips
Calculator	Index cards	Writing paper
Clock	Comfortable chair	Surge protector

Cutting Board:

1. Put an asterisk (*) near the objects that you now own.
2. Put an exclamation point (!) next to the ones that you feel you should own.
3. Write down any other objects you will be needing or wanting to have in your dissertation kitchen/workspace:_____

Pick Your Repast [Choose Your Topic]

1/2 c.   "P"ossess Knowledge of What a Dissertation Is and Is Not

1 c.   "I"dentify Your Cooking (Researching) Style

1/2 c.   "C"lassify Yourself Professionally

1 c.   "K"(c)onduct the ROC Bottom Test

1/2 c. "P"osses Knowledge of What a Dissertation Is and Is Not

Before you go through the process of selecting a dissertation project and topic, it would behoove you to keep in mind that a dissertation is not necessarily:

1.   A Nobel Prize project.
2.   The final answer to a pressing problem.
3.   The last research paper that you will write.
4.   About the "hottest" topic in your field.
5.   Going to excite all your friends.

What then is a dissertation (we hear you cry)? A dissertation is a formal research project usually required for an advanced degree which you:

1.   Can "put your arms around." In a couple of minutes you could tell someone in your profession, as well as in another profession, what it is about.
2.   Already know a great deal about, including where it will fit into a larger picture.
3.   Are truly concerned and curious about.
4.   Could conceivably present at a professional meeting.
5.   Are willing to dedicate a great deal of time to complete.
6.   Can call your own.
7.   Can proclaim is researchable, original, and contributory to your profession (see (K)conduct a ROC bottom test).
8.   Will know when you have completed, i.e. ascertained enough information to have accepted or not accepted your research questions or hypotheses.

1 c. "I"dentifying Your Cooking (Research) Style

Choosing Your Research Project/Topic—What Type of Cook (Researcher) Are You?

Most of us have our own unique style of inquiry. Some styles embody the traditional norms of science while others exemplify non-traditional norms. There is no one right or wrong way to investigate a problem per se, but if you have a very strong research style, you might find it frustrating to work on a project that is designed for a different type of researcher. A dissertation topic should be an original contribution to scholarly research that fills a void in the literature and extends prior knowledge. A dissertation can replicate a study in a different environment or time or develop a new theory. Regardless of its intent, you should find a project that you are passionate about working diligently on.

Note: It is important to keep in mind that in doing research there is room for the daring, speculative, inventive spirit who creates new theories or tries bold, imaginative experiments, as well as for the cautious, critical spirit who examines theories searchingly and patiently designs

16

experiments requiring complete attention to detail. There are researchers who prefer the precision of mathematics and those who prefer the color of words; those who prefer to deal with human beings and human problems and others who prefer to work with computers or microscopes. However, according to Goldstein and Goldstein in their book *How We Know* (1985), "for all there should be the same goal—the joy and excitement of discovery and the same outcome—knowledge."

On the cutting board that follows you will find a "typology" of major ways in which people make inquiries, adapted from Mitroff and Kilmann's *Methodological Approaches to Social Science* (1978).

Answer each question and record your answers in the spaces provided. This will give you an opportunity to discover what method(s) of doing research would work well for you.

For Your Information and Education

Although there are many different ways to classify types of scientific thinking, C. G. Jung's classification has been chosen because it takes into account both affect (feeling) and cognition (thinking).

Cutting Board:

Read each statement below, and indicate on the accompanying Likert-type scale how strongly you agree with each declaration.

1. T: To truly understand the AIDS epidemic, one must ascertain the "Truth" about AIDS. A researcher must look at the data and make recommendations for further study based on these findings. The researcher should not base conclusions on information that is obtained through subjective means or anecdotal stories or rely too heavily on his/her personal feelings.

disagree totally			agree totally	
1	2	3	4	T = _2_

2. F: To truly understand the AIDS epidemic, one must look at the individuals afflicted with the disease and note the similarities and differences that exist among them. Recommendations for further study should be based on the immediate needs of those individuals as well as how the researcher feels he/she could best be personally involved.

disagree totally			agree totally	
1	2	3	4	F = _3_

3. S: To deal with environmental problems, one should look at the methods available and determine what is the most practical way to solve these problems now, and not spend the time on some "vague" plan in the unspecified future.

disagree totally			agree totally	
1	2	3	4	S = _2_

4. I: To deal with environmental problems, one should look at all the possibilities that exist now and, more importantly, could exist, and take a broad, long-range view of the situation. A quick fix to the problem should be avoided.

disagree totally			agree totally	
1	2	3	4	I = __3__

To discover your research typology:

1. Enter your T, F, I, and S numbers in the spaces provided.
2. Fill in the table by computing the sums of T + I in cell I, T + S in cell II, S + F in cell III, and I + F in cell IV.
3. Your research style(s) is(are) the cell(s) with the largest sum.
4. Underline the style(s) with the largest sum.

	T-value: __2__	F-value: __3__
I-value: __3__	I. ~~8~~ 5	IV. ~~8~~ 6
S-value: __2__	II. 4	III. 5

I. Conceptual Theorist   II. Analytical Scientist
III. Particular Humanist   IV. <u>Conceptual Humanist</u>

Note: If you have the luxury of selecting your own faculty advisor(s), you might want to determine what type of researcher(s) they are. Offer to conduct this test with potential advisors to see if you have compatible research styles.

What follows is a description of the archetype associated with each of the research styles above. See if the research style you have underlined suits your style of inquiry.

I. **Conceptual Theorist.** This type of researcher believes in TOE, i.e., The Theory of Everything. A conceptual theorist is holistic and imaginative. He/she believes in multiple causations and the development of a coherent-testable framework complemented with large-scale correlation. Science holds some privilege in this type of thinking, but it is not the only way that a conceptual theorist views a problem. Motto: Conflict is an important characteristic of research and should not be dismissed. Conflict is vital to the development of both methods and theories.

II. **Analytical Scientist.** This type of researcher prefers exactness, precision, and unambiguous situations. Science is paramount and exact in this type of thinking. The analytical scientist sees science as ruled by nature. The ideal experiment is one where all the variables are controlled. Motto: In order to label something a scientific theory, it must be cast into a logical form so that given the proper antecedent conditions (X, A), one can make the valid deduction (Y). Otherwise, it is non-scientific.

III. **Particular Humanist.** This type of researcher prefers personal knowledge to rational knowledge. Science is not privileged in this type of thinking and is subordinate to other disciplines such as poetry and literature. The particular humanist believes that humans are too complex to study as a whole. Motto: It is absurd to think that science has remained immune to outside influences. The challenge is to develop a methodology of science that does justice not only to the humanity of the subjects studied but to the researcher as well. Only a person who is passionately involved in his/her research can make a difference.

(IV.) **Conceptual Humanist.** This type of researcher prefers holistic knowledge. Science has no special privilege in this type of thinking. Knowledge exists only to better humanity. To further understand humanity, a conceptual humanist believes, one must study human behavior and constantly develop new theories based on these observations. Motto: The question is not "Is storytelling science?" but "Can science learn to tell a good story?"

Below are research topics that would likely appeal to the people with archetypes described above who wish to conduct an investigation of the relationship between smoking and health. Read each research topic and see if the research topic described for your archetype appeals to you.

If asked to choose a research topic on smoking and health: Topics of Most Interest:

I.   Determine the correlation between smoking and diseases, smoking and personality types, why people smoke, and as many multiple correlations as one can ascertain between smoking and other factors.

II.   Determine definitively if cigarette smoking causes cancer. Simulate smoking in laboratory animals and determine if cancer is caused.

III. Study a smoker and determine why this person started smoking and any ill effects that smoking has. Have cancer patients who have smoked keep a diary and study their feelings and concerns.

IV.   Survey ex-smokers and determine the most effective ways each person was able to stop smoking.

Cutting Board:

1.   Which of these studies appealed to you the most? _____
2.   Which appealed to you the least?_____
3.   Did you approve of the study defined for your archetype? _____ Explain:

_____

4.   Keep this knowledge in mind when you select your dissertation topic.

1/2 c. "C"lassify Yourself Professionally

Now that you have an idea of what your research style is, it is important that you take the time to objectively classify yourself within your profession. To choose a project that will sustain your enthusiasm, help you remain dedicated, and enable you to see to fruition in a reasonable amount of time, requires a heavy dash of knowing who you are professionally and what has attracted you to your discipline.

By using a process in which you will be going from a broad to a narrow perspective, you will be able to discern a researchable project or projects that you are very capable of pursuing with vigor. Be aware, however, that once you are immersed in your research, you might decide to change or modify your focus. Be assured that each time you modify your study, you will be more knowledgeable and have fewer obstacles to overcome. One excellent way to find a topic is to network with other researchers around the globe. With the Internet this can be easily accomplished by joining listservs. A review of the literature often reveals a topic worthy of researching. Also, most dissertations have a section: Recommendations for Future Research. This could be another excellent way to find THE problem you wish to work on.

The cutting board that follows can also assist you in formulating a dissertation topic. Dr. M. will share with you how she obtained her dissertation topic. You will be referred to as Dr. I during this exploratory activity. (Remember to keep in mind what a dissertation is and is not and what your research typology told you about how you like to investigate a problem.)

Cutting Board:

1. What is (are) your professional role(s) or the role that you are seeking? (E.g., are you an educator, doctor, nurse, administrator, actress, lawyer, political scientist, media person, anthropologist, engineer, computer scientist, psychologist, sociologist?)
   Dr. M. is an educator.
   Dr. I. is _____ educ/anthro _____
2. What is (are) your principal area(s) of interest (PI) or your subspecialty within your profession?
   Dr. M. is a mathematics educator and consultant.
   Dr. I. is _____
3. What area(s) of your PI are you most enthusiastic and/or involved with? (What made you decide to go into this profession?)
   Dr. M. is interested in and involved with mathematics anxiety, technology in the classroom, teacher training, statistics, and the future of mathematics education. She enjoys mathematics and believes that everyone can be successful in mathematics if they are given the opportunity to do math their way.
   Dr. I. is interested in and involved with: _____
   The reasons why Dr. I chose this profession are: _____
4. What are some problems that you are interested in that you believe need some "new light," or need to be looked at critically for the first time?
   Dr. M. believes that calculators were not being used in the elementary school classroom because of the anxiety of elementary school teachers.
   Dr. I. believes that: _____
5. Restate the most pressing problem you have described using a preferred style of inquiry:
   Dr. M. (a conceptual theorist): What is the relationship between mathematics anxiety and lack of calculator use in the classroom?
   Dr. I. _____
6. Select a title (topic) based on this problem:
   Dr. M. *The Wasted Resource: Attitudinal problems in calculator use among elementary school teachers*.
   Dr. I. _____

Fantastic! You have yourself a research topic, Dr. I. Now, before you start your celebration, you will need to K(c)onduct the ROC bottom test to see if the topic you have selected has the following attributes: R(esearchability), O(riginality), and if it is C(ontributory).

1 c. "K"(c)onduct the ROC Bottom Test

      1/3 c. "R"esearchability

      1/3 c. "O"riginality

      1/3 c. "C"ontributory

1/3 c. "R"esearchability

Use the cutting board which follows to test whether your topic is researchable. You should be able to answer "YES" to the majority of questions below.

If this is not the case then you might want to go **FISH**, Find Interest Somewhere Hence. (You would probably not want to prepare a dinner of an exotic Asian fish that you could not obtain to a group of vegetarians who would not eat this fish even if you somehow managed to obtain it. Would you?)

Cutting Board:

1. Are there textbooks that deal with this topic? _____
2. Are there journals or periodicals that deal with this topic? _____
3. Are there Web Sites you can visit to obtain information? _____
4. Can you obtain access to files you might need? _____
5. Can you access a sample of your population or the population itself? _____
6. Will you know when you have obtained the information you are seeking? _____
7. Can you obtain authorization to do your research? _____
8. Can you obtain the support of people who are essential to your project? _____

1/3 c. "O"riginality

A "YES" to one or more questions on the cutting board below will satisfy the "O" requirement and indicate that your topic has originality. If all the answers are no's, you might want to go FISH.

Cutting Board:

1. Will this study provide some new way to look at an existing problem?
2. Will this be a missing piece to an existing problem?
3. Is this a new contradiction to an accepted point of view?
4. Is this a new way to look at a historical work?
5. Is this a recommendation from a published study?
6. Is this a repetitive study using a different population or another look at a population studied after the passage of time?
7. Is this a new approach to an old problem?
8. Will this be the first time a program or treatment is being evaluated in this manner?

1/3 c. "C"ontributory

A "YES" to at least one question on the cutting board below will satisfy the "C" requirement and indicate that your research will be contributory. If all the answers are no's, you might want to go **FISH.**

Cutting Board:

1.   Is there a need in your profession to know the results of this study?
2.   Will there be people in your profession or people who plan to enter this profession who will need the information that this study will ascertain?
3.   Will people outside of your profession gain new insight into something in your profession after this study is complete?
4.   Will some members of society, or society at large, suffer if this study is NOT done?

Once you have passed the **ROC** bottom test you will have made a major step toward obtaining your goal. Congratulations! You should feel proud and happy.

Note: A doctoral dissertation or formal research project must have a very high level of quality and integrity. The entire research project and paper must be clear, lucid, logical, have an appropriate theoretical base, contain appropriate statistical analysis (if needed), and have proper citations.

Now that you have nailed down your topic, you will need to develop a solid problem statement. When this major task is accomplished, put this statement in your working environment and carry a copy of it with you whenever you are working on your dissertation. It is important to never lose sight of what you are researching and why you are conducting this research.

Cutting Board:

In bold print write out your research topic again in the space below: _____

_____

The heart of a doctoral dissertation, and most formal research projects, is the PROBLEM STATEMENT. This is the place where most assessors go first to understand and appraise the merits of your proposal or your research. After reading the problem statement, the reader will know why you are doing (did) this study and be convinced of its importance. In 250 words or less (about 1–3 paragraphs) you need to convince the reader that this study must (had to) be done!

The reason that you do a doctoral dissertation or formal research is because society, or one of its institutions, has some pressing problem that needs closer attention. The problem statement delineates this problem while hinting at the nature of the study—correlation, evaluative, historical, experimental—that is, how you will (did) solve the problem.

Once a clear and lucid problem statement is formed all the research you put into your dissertation should be focused on obtaining a solution. You will be judged by the degree to which you find the answer to the problem you pose and, thus, achieve your purpose.

Note: A problem that results in a "yes" or "no" answer is not suitable for formal research. For example, the problem: to determine if homework is beneficial for high school students is not appropriate for scholarly research, but the researcher can form a suitable problem statement around this topic with a bit of finesse with the statement: to determine wherein lie the benefits of homework to high school students, if they exist. You must say precisely what you mean in as concise a manner as possible.

A problem statement that is too narrowly focused may direct the researcher only toward trivia. A statement that is too broad may not adequately delineate the relationships or concepts involved in the study. Development of a well-constructed problem statement leads to the logical outgrowth of well-constructed research questions and/or hypotheses, and supports all aspects of a research project.

Many researchers have difficulty formulating a succinct problem statement. The following activity can assist you in preparing a "delectable" problem statement. Further suggestions are offered in Phase 3.

Cutting Board:

By answering the following questions, you will be able to develop a first rate problem statement. Fill in the blanks as best you can, and from these "ingredients" try to "cook up" a "delicious" problem statement.

1. What is the problem?_____
2. Where is this problem found (what profession(s), sub-specialty)? [This will help in your literature review.] _____
3. What are some of the ill effects of this problem on society at large and/or some subset of society? [This will help with your background section.] _____
4. Why are you interested in this problem? [This will help in your significance statement.] Why would someone else be interested in this problem?

   _____
5. Who is affected? What group would care about this problem? [This will help define the sample and population, and help define significance.] What part of this problem can this study help solve? _____
6. How can this study help? (Assist in making wiser choices, debunk a myth.) [This will help define your purpose and significance.] _____
7. Of what professional value will the research be? (Clarify an ambiguous point or theory, look at a new aspect of a problem, aid in an important decision-making process. . . .) [This helps with the purpose and significance.] What journal would be interested in publishing this study?

   _____
8. What needs to be done? (Analyze, describe, evaluate, test, understand, determine . . .) [This will help decide the methodology (ies) and instruments to be used.]

   _____

9. What topics, subjects, issues are involved? (Stock market, drugs, violence, language development, assessment, euthanasia. . . .) [This will help in the literature review.]

_____

10. How does the study relate to the development or the refinement of theory? [This will help with your theoretical framework.] _____

11. What will result from this study? (Clarify, debunk, relieve, assist create, recommend. . . .) [This will help in interpreting the results.] _____

12. What harm would (could) be done if this study was NOT done? _____

13. *Optional:* What has already been done about it? What hasn't been done? Who is requesting such a study? [This will help with your literature review.]

_____

In big and bold letters, write your problem statement in the space below. Be aware that this might be modified a bit when you get to Phase 3.

_____

Keep this with you whenever you are conducting your research!

Classify Your Repast—What's Cooking? [Identify Your Study]

The value of research is defined by how the work underway fits into the overall context of the theory or paradigm being researched. Thus, researchers must be fully cognizant of why they are doing what they are doing and what they expect the return on their efforts to be.

Gilovitch—How What We Know Isn't So (1991)

Below you will find a sampling of different types of research methodologies. This list is by no means conclusive or exhaustive but should offer you a variety of ways to classify your research. Once you have determined what type of research you will be conducting it might be wise to find textbooks and journal articles that deal with that particular methodology in detail so that you will be aware of the intricacies of applying that methodology to your study.

One common perspective for viewing a research project is that of time. We will examine clusters of methodologies based on past, present, and future perspectives.

A	B
Past	**Present**
Historical	Developmental
Content Analysis	Descriptive
	Pure/Basic/Experimental
	Quasi-Experimental

C	D
Future	**Nouveau Cuisine**
Action	Heuristic
Applied	Holistic
Evaluative	Grounded Theory
Causal-Comparative	Ethnographic
Correlational	Delphi
Case Study	
Phenomenological	

Now that you have selected your topic, you are in an excellent position to determine "what's cooking." You are now ready to ascertain what type of a research study you will be conducting. Your research methodology refers to the broad perspective from which you will view the problem, make the investigation, and draw inferences.

Although no single research methodology is likely to describe each aspect of the problem you are planning to investigate, there are most likely general categories into which your study will fall. There is no universal standard for categorizing research designs, and different authors may change names of designs in their discussions of them. Thus what is shown here is intended to be more informative than exhaustive. This lack of universalism also causes problems when critiquing research, as many published studies do not identify the design used. Selecting an appropriate design for a study involves following a logical thought process. A calculating mind is required to explore all possible consequences of using a particular design in a study.

Choose Your Methodology Wisely

Don't be too quick in running away from using a quantitative methodology because you fear the use of statistics. A qualitative approach to research can yield new and exciting understandings, but it should not be undertaken because of a fear of quantitative research. A well-designed quantitative research study can often be accomplished in very clear and direct ways. A similar study of a qualitative nature usually requires considerably more time and a burden to create new paths for analysis where previously no path had existed. Choose your methodology wisely!

After reading the descriptions below, find the classification that best describes the nature of your study. We will primarily use problems associated with low socio-economic class and its relation to education—an example to show how each of these methodologies could analyze the same problem.

Use the cutting board after each example to demonstrate how the problem you are investigating could be resolved with each methodology.

Past Perspective

If you are primarily interested in past events or factors in the past that have contributed to the problem you are researching, then your methodology will likely be historical or causal-comparative.

Historical Research

The researcher looks back at significant events in the relatively distant past and seeks, by gathering and analyzing contemporary descriptions of the event, to provide a coherent and objective picture of what happened. The historical researcher deals with the meaning of events. There is usually a reconstruction of the past in relation to a particular theory or conceptual scheme. The heart of this research is the interpretation of facts and events to determine not just what happened, but why they happened. The data of historical research are subject to two types of evaluation: to determine if a document is authentic, or, if indeed it is authentic, what the document means. The researcher is concerned with external or internal evidence and subjects the data to external or internal criticism.

Example: A study of 19th century teaching practices with children of low socio-economic class using teacher diaries as primary sources.

Cutting Board:

Content Analysis

The researcher examines a class of social artifacts, typically written documents. Topics appropriate for content analysis include: any form of communication answering who says what? to whom? why? how? with what effect? This is an unobtrusive method of doing research, but it is limited to recorded information. Coding is used to transform raw data into standardized, quantitative form. Data are analyzed through the use of official or quasi-official statistics.

Content analysis examines words or phrases within a wide range of texts, including books, book chapters, essays, interviews, and speeches as well as informal conversation and headlines. By examining the presence or repetition of certain words and phrases in these texts, a researcher is able to make inferences about the philosophical assumptions of a writer, a written piece, the audience for which the piece is written, and even the culture and time in which the text is embedded. Due to its wide array of applications, researchers in literature and rhetoric, marketing, psychology and cognitive science, as well as many other fields, use content analysis.

Example: Documents from Title I programs are analyzed over a ten-year period to determine any patterns or trends in entitlements.

Cutting Board:

Present Perspective

If your study adopts a viewpoint that is in the present time, then you will likely be examining a phenomenon as it occurs with a view to understanding its nature, organization, and/or the way it changes.

Developmental Research

The researcher examines patterns and sequences of growth and change over time. This research can be done as a longitudinal study (the same group examined over a period of time) or as a cross-sectional study (different groups examined at the same time which might represent different ages or other classifications). Check out the following URL to see studies using developmental research techniques: *http://www.psy.miami.edu/Child/Applied/child_applied_research.html*

Example: A group of freshman students from a "high risk" school are studied to examine the factors that affect their ability to graduate in four years.

Cutting Board:

Descriptive Research

The researcher makes a systematic analysis and description of the facts and characteristics of a given population or event of interest. The purpose of this form of research is to provide a detailed and accurate picture of the phenomenon as a means of generating hypotheses and pinpointing areas of needed improvements. Descriptive studies are designed to gain more information about a particular characteristic within a particular field of study. A descriptive study may be used to develop theory, identify problems with current practice, justify current practice, make judgments, or identify what others in similar situations may be doing. There is no manipulation of variables and no attempt to establish causality.

Example: A needs assessment study of an urban ghetto is carried out as a preliminary step toward the establishment of a special pre-school program for children of low socio-economic status.

Cutting Board:

Correlational Research

The researcher investigates one or more characteristic of a group in order to discover the extent to which the characteristics vary together. Descriptive and correlational studies examine variables in their natural environments and do not include researcher-imposed treatments. Correlational studies display the relationships among variables by such techniques as cross-tabulation and correlations. Correlational studies are also known as ex post facto studies. This literally means "from after the fact." The term is used to identify that the research in question has been conducted after the variations in the independent variable has occurred naturally.

The basic purpose of this form of study is to determine the relationship between variables. However the significant difference from experimental and quasi-experimental design is that causality cannot be established due to lack of manipulation of independent variables. "Correlation does not prove Causation." In studying the relationship between smoking and cancer, the researcher begins with a sample of those who have already developed the disease and a sample of those who have not. The researcher then looks for differences between the two groups in antecedents, behaviors, or conditions such as smoking habits

Example: The relationship between socio-economic status and school achievement of a group of urban ghetto children is examined.

Cutting Board:

Causal-Comparative Research

The researcher looks at present characteristics of a problem, views them as the result of past causal factors and tries, by examining those past factors, to discover the causes, critical relationships, and meanings suggested by a characteristic. Usually two or more groups are compared using this characteristic.

Causal-comparative and correlational methods are similar in that both are nonexperimental methods since they lack manipulation of an independent variable which is under the control of the experimenter, and random assignment of participants is not possible. This implies that variables need to be observed as they occur naturalistically. As a result, the key and omnipresent problem in nonexperimental research is that an observed relationship between an independent variable and a dependent variable may be spurious. That is, the relationship might not be causal but instead the result of the operation of a third variable.

Causal-comparative research generally includes a categorical independent and/or dependent variable (hence the word "comparative" implying a group comparison) while correlational research only includes quantitative variables. Causal-comparative studies attempt to establish cause-effect relationships, correlational studies do not. Correlational research attempts to determine whether, and to what degree, a relationship exists between two or more quantifiable variables. Causal-comparative is similar to experimental research since both usually involve a comparison of groups, and an attempt is made to establish cause-effect relationships. The main purpose of a correlational study is to determine relationships between variables, or to use relationships in making predictions.

Example: Comparison of the socio-economic status of a high-achieving group of children and a low-achieving group of children to ascertain whether and to what extent socio-economic status influences school performance.

Cutting Board:

28

Pure/Basic/Experimental Research

Check out *http://www.fortunecity.com/greenfield/grizzly/432/rra2.htm*

This type of research is typically oriented toward the development of theories by discovering broad generalization based on careful analysis of a sample of the population being studied. It usually follows a scientific type of inquiry emphasizing a rigorous, structured type of analysis in each of the research stages.

The paradigm for scientific method in research is the true experiment or randomized control trial. Experimental designs are set up to allow the greatest amount of control possible so that causality may be examined closely. The three essential elements of experimental design are:

- **Manipulation:** The researcher does something to at least some of the participants in the research.
- **Control:** The experimenter introduces one or more controls over the experimental situation.
- **Randomization:** The experimenter assigns participants to different groups on a random basis (adapted from Polit & Hungler 4th Edn., 1991).

The classic example is the before/after design or pre-test/post-test design. This is perhaps the most commonly used experimental design. Comparison of pre-test scores allows the researcher to evaluate how effective the randomization of the sample is in providing equivalent groups. The treatment is fully under control of the researcher. The dependent variable is measured twice during the study (before and after the manipulation of the independent variable).

There are many texts that specifically address experimental methods. If you are intending to conduct an experimental study, you should thoroughly familiarize yourself with the procedures.

The following checklist of questions was adapted from Creswell (1994).

Questions to consider when designing an experimental study:

- Who are the subjects in the study, and to what population do these subjects belong?
- How were the subjects or participants selected?
- Was a random selection procedure used?
- Will the subjects be matched in some form?
- What will be the division of subjects in the experimental and the control groups?

The ideal is to ensure that each individual, event, observation, etc. has an equal chance of being selected from the population. A deliberate or convenience sample may be selected when circumstances warrant, such as an entire classroom or an entire organization. When volunteers participate in a study, this would be defined as a deliberate or convenience sample, since it may not be representative. Always be clear on how your sample is taken.

- What are the independent variables (predictors) in the study and how will they be measured?
- How many times will they be measured?
- What are the dependent variables (that being predicted)? Be sure they are identified.

Remember that it is the IV or independent variables (x) that cause or influence an outcome on the DV or dependent variable (y). As Creswell (1991) stated it, "the dependent variable is the response or the criterion variable presumed to be caused or influenced by the independent treatment conditions." The independent variables are those variables that provide the "treatment" or those variables that act as "factors" in an experiment. These independentvariablesareunder the control of the researcher and are "manipulated" by the researcher in conducting the experiment.

Creswell cites Rosnow (1991) in suggesting that there are three prototype outcome measures in experiments. They include the general outcome measures as: (1) the direction of the observed changes; (2) the amount, volume, quantity, etc. of the change; and (3) the "ease" with which the change is effected. This may be an over simplification; nevertheless, it helps to provide a general orientation as to outcome measures.

- What instruments will be used to measure the outcomes?
- Why was the particular instrument chosen?
- Did you design the instrument or did another person develop it?
- What procedural steps are taken in your experimental study regarding random assignments of subjects to groups, the collection of demographic information, the administration of a pre-test or pilot experiment, etc.?
- What statistics will be used to analyze the data?
- What assumptions need to be made before you can use the statistical test?

Indicate whether the instrument(s) selected have an established validity and reliability, using the same criteria as for survey instruments. Consider seeking expert advice on statistical analysis, if you have limited knowledge about the application and use of statistical tests. Keep in mind, however, that you ultimately must understand the nature, purpose, and intended use of the statistical tests in your study. Thus, the lengthy discussion of statistical analysis in *The Dissertation and Research Cookbook* should be studied and understood. Questions often arise in the oral presentation of dissertation proposals and in the oral presentation (or final defense) of the dissertation itself about the selection of statistical tests. You need to be aware of why a test was chosen and what assumptions are essential to its use.

When experimental research is applied to the social sciences, the researcher and subjects interact in such a way that the subjects make no contribution to formulating the propositions that purport to be about them or to be based on their sayings or doings. The inquiry is all on the side of the researcher, and the action being inquired into is all on the side of the subject.

The analytical scientist's basic drive is toward certainty, that is precision, accuracy, and reliability. In its simplest form, the experimental method attempts to control the entire research situation. The matter of control is basic to this method. The researcher seeks two matched groups and gives one the "experimental treatment" and the other receives either no treatment or a placebo. Any endeavor that cannot be subjected to this type of reasoning is either suppressed, devalued, or set aside.

In some studies the dependent variable cannot be measured before the treatment. For example, we cannot effectively measure the response to interventions designed to control nausea from chemotherapy prior to the beginning of treatment. Here we would use an approach known as the post-test-only design. We may also wish to use this approach where pre-test sensitization may occur. Subject's post-test response may be partly due to learning from, or as a reaction to, the pre-test. In these instances the pre-test phase can be eliminated, however doing so removes the possibility of applying some very powerful statistical analysis.

Example: Two groups of low socio-economic class children are randomly assigned to either an experimental enrichment program prior to entering school, or a control group of traditional pre-school play. Comparison is made of their subsequent school performances to determine whether such enrichment influences achievement.

Quasi-Experimental Design

Check out: *http://www.fortunecity.com/greenfield/grizzly/432/rra2.htm#quasi*
Quasi-experimental designs were developed to provide alternate means for examining cau-sality in situations which were not conducive to experimental control. The designs have been developed to control as many threats to validity as possible in situations where at least one of the three elements of true experimental research is lacking (i.e., manipulation, randomization, control group).

There are many types of quasi-experimental design (see Burns & Grove, 1993, pp. 305–316). Most are adaptations of experimental designs where one of the three elements is missing.

Example: The researcher uses groups (control and treatment) that have evolved naturally in some way, say a group of prodigious young musicians, rather than being randomly selected to determine parental involvement in their music. This is a quasi-experimental approach using non-equivalent control groups.

Case Study

The case study method refers to descriptive research based on a real-life situation, problem, or incident and cases describing situations calling for analysis, planning, decision-making, and/or action with boundaries established by the researcher. Case study research is a type of qualitative research that concentrates on a single unit or entity, with boundaries established by the researcher (Lichtman, Merilyn; Taylor, Satomi Izumi, 1993).

Case study research is often used when the questions are how and why, rather than what and how many, and when particularistic, descriptive, heuristic, and inductive phenomena are considered. Sudzina and Kilbane (1992) maintain that the method requires that every attempt be made to provide an unbiased, multidimensional perspective in presenting the case and arriving at solutions. The case study is dependent upon the ability to apply techniques which are multimodal to situations.

According to Goetz and LeCompte (1984) there are seven points in the case study process where important theoretical decisions need to be made: focus and purpose; research design; choice of subjects; settings and context; the role of the researcher; data collection strategies; data analysis methods; findings and interpretations. Case studies use inductive logic to discover the reality behind the data collected through the study.

Example: A high school in a low socio-economic area is studied to gather data for an analysis of attitudes and practices as they relate to drug education.

Phenomenology

This type of research has its roots in existentialism. Data are structured by the subjects' descriptions of the experiences and the researcher's interpretation of the descriptions. Interview is the most common instrument of data collection, which means that the quality of the data depends on the subjects' written and verbal skills. The researcher, in turn, must depend heavily on his/her intuitive skills. It is usually wise for the researcher to frame his/her own feelings, attitudes, biases, and understandings of the phenomenon prior to conducting a phenomenological study.

Phenomenology is a 20th-century philosophical movement dedicated to describing the structures of experience as they present themselves to consciousness, without recourse to theory, deduction, or assumptions from other disciplines such as the natural sciences. Phenomenology is both a philosophy and a research method. The purpose of phenomenological research is to describe experiences as they are lived in phenomenological terms (i.e., to capture the "lived experience" of study participants). The philosophers from which phenomenology emerged include Husserl, Kierkegaard, Heidegger, and Jean Paul Sartre.

Phenomenologists view the person as integral with the environment. The focus of phenomenological research is people's experience in regard to a phenomenon and how they interpret their experiences. Phenomenologists agree that there is not a single reality; each individual has his or her own reality. This is considered true even of the researcher's experience in collecting data and analyzing it. "Truth is an interpretation of some phenomenon; the more shared that interpretation is the more factual it seems to be, yet it remains temporal and cultural" (Munhall, 1989).

There are four aspects of the human experience, which are of interest to the phenomenological researcher:

1. Lived Space (Spatiality)
2. Lived Body (Corporeality)
3. Lived Human Relationships (Relationality)
4. Lived Time (Temporality)

All of these aspects are taken into consideration—we must be aware that people see different realities in different situations, in the company of different people, and at different times. The feelings expressed about one's life in an interview given at a certain time may be very different from those given at another time.

The broad question that phenomenologists want answered is "What is the meaning of one's lived experience?" The only reliable source of information to answer this question is the person. Understanding human behavior or experience requires that the person interpret the action or experience for the researcher, and then the researcher must interpret the explanation provided by the person.

The first step in conducting a phenomenological study is to identify the phenomenon to explore. Next, the researcher will develop the research question. Two factors need to be considered in developing the research question:

- What are the necessary constituents of this feeling or experience?
- What does the existence of this feeling or experience indicate concerning the nature of the human being?

After developing the research question, the researcher identifies the sources of the phenomenon being studied and from these sources seeks individuals who are willing to describe their experience(s) with the phenomenon in question. These individuals must understand and be willing to express their inner feelings and describe any physiological experiences that occur with the feelings.

Data are collected through a variety of means: observation, interactive interviews, videotape and written descriptions by subjects. Typically, the data are collected by in-depth conversations in which the researcher and the subject (informant) are fully interactive. Analysis begins when the first data are collected. This analysis will guide decisions related to further data collection. The meanings attached to the data are expressed within the phenomenological philosophy. The outcome of analysis is a theoretical statement responding to the research question. The statement is validated by examples of the data, often direct quotes from the subjects. More information on phenomenology is available at *http://www.connect.net/ron/phenom.html.*

Example: A researcher spends several months at an inner-city high school to determine the perceptions of the teachers and students with respect to school policies.

Cutting Board:

Future Perspective

If your prime interest is the future, in studying a current situation for the purpose of contributing to a decision about it, changing it, or establishing a policy about it, you will probably use one of the following research methodologies.

Applied or Evaluative Research

This type of research is concerned primarily with the application of new knowledge for the solution of day-to-day problems. The knowledge obtained is thus contextual. Its purpose is to improve a process by testing theoretical constructs in actual situations. In medical research a cardiologist might monitor a group of heart disease patients to see if the diet prescribed by the American Heart Association is truly effective. A great deal of social research fits into this category for it attempts to establish whether various organizations and institutions are fulfilling their purpose. The relationship between researcher and subject is one of expert and client.

Many social action programs have been researched in this manner. It highlights the symbols of measurement and scientific neutrality but attempts to minimize the influence of the behavioral science perspective.

Example: An income-enhanced program for raising the socio-economic status of parents of pre-school children is evaluated for its effects upon school performance of children.

Cutting Board:

Action Research

This is a type of applied research which is more concerned with immediate application, rather than the development of a theory. It focuses on specific problems in a particular situation and usually involves those who can immediately create change. Bogdan and Biklen (1992) describe action research as a systematic collection of information that is designed to bring about social change. This kind of research allows that there could be more than one right way to develop solutions to problems.

The beginnings of "action research" date back to Lewin (1946). In his study of "group decision and social change," he used his model to describe how to change people's relationship to food. His research consisted of analysis, fact-finding, conceptualization, planning, execution, more fact-finding, conceptualization, etc. Marrow (1969) saw the Lewin model as a means of studying subjects through changing them and seeing the effect. This type of inquiry is based on the belief that in order to gain insight into a process one must introduce a change and then observe its variable effects and new dynamics.

Action research is neither quantitative nor qualitative research. It has been argued that it is more of a tool for change than true research. Action research "is a way of doing research and working on solving a problem at the same time" (Cormack, 1991, p. 155).

The method was developed to allow researcher and participants to work together to analyze social systems with a view to changing them. In other words, to achieve specific goals. It is seen as a community based method and has frequently been employed in a wide range of settings: from schools and health clinics to businesses and industry.

The approach may include doing some base line measures using questionnaires, observation, or other research methods as an assessment of the problem. Objectives are then set and decisions made about how to bring about a change. When change plans are put into action progress is monitored, changing the plans as necessary or appropriate. Once the change has been implemented, a final assessment is made and conclusions drawn, accompanied by the writing of a report on the project for those involved or for dissemination to others.

Therefore, action research "is a process containing both investigation and the use of its findings" (Smith, 1986, cited by Cormack, 1991, p. 155). The role of the researcher is to assist practitioners in taking control of and changing their own work.

Action research has the following characteristics:

1. Has an educational function.
2. Deals with individuals as members of social groups.
3. Is problem focused, context specific, and future orientated.
4. Involves a change intervention.
5. Aims at improvement and involvement.
6. Involves a cyclic process in which research, action, and evaluation are interlinked.
7. Is found in a research relationship where those involved are participants in the change process.

The phrase Look, Think, Act has been used by Stringer (1996) in the book *Action Research: A Handbook for Practitioners.*

To conduct action research involves identifying the problem, discussing the problem practitioners, conducting a thorough search of the literature, re-defining the problem, selecting an evaluation model, implementing a change, collecting data, receiving feedback, making recommendations, and disseminating the results to a larger audience.

Example: A program in which teachers are given in-service workshops and new materials to use with low socio-economic status children is implemented in two pilot schools, evaluated as it progresses, and continually modified to become more effective.

Cutting Board:

"Nouveau Cuisine"

Below is a list of some non-traditional meals that have been successfully served at modern day banquets.

Heuristic Research

In action research, hypotheses are being created and tested, whereas in heuristic research, the investigator encourages individuals to discover their own hypotheses in relation to a problem and decide on methods which would enable them to investigate further on their own.

In heuristic research, the emphasis is on personal commitment rather than linear methodologies. Its purpose is to describe a meaningful pattern as it exists in the universe without any pre-designed plan, thus eliminating suggestive speculation. This type of research intrinsically tends to be more open ended than most.

For Your Information and Education

Clark Moustakas (1961) did a study on loneliness based on his own personal experiences, and after its publication, several "lonely" people picked up on his work and furthered the study. He then published their studies so that others could gain more insight into this situation.

Moustakas felt this type of "heuristic research" recognizes the significance of inner searching for deeper awareness. He saw this approach as an integration of searching, studying, and as an openness to new experiences, intuition, and process. Critics of heuristic research feel that it is just an elaboration of the problem stage of research and should not be construed as the research itself.

Example: An adult coming from a low socio-economic class who obtains a Ph.D. and seeks out other such people, asking them a series of questions in order to point out the similarities and differences in their responses.

Cutting Board:

In holistic research, qualities of traditional research, such as a systematic inquiry and rigorous search for the truth, are given the same priority as relevancy, intuition, and human dignity.

Whereas traditional research relies almost exclusively on references to previously peer-reviewed studies, holistic research often gives details of political standpoints, current works, and relationships from a variety of sources. Generally, you would choose this type of research methodology if you feel a need for exploring all methods of inquiry including the use of fictional literature, art, and music, where applicable, or if you are attempting to create a new theory or identify a new problem.

Holistic researchers feel that the tendency of traditional researchers to rely heavily on test results and to over-specialize is a serious shortcoming which trivializes people and shows little humility. Maslow (1970) has stated that "if you prod at people like things they won't let you know them."

For Your Information and Education

If you choose one of the non-traditional research methodologies, you might wish to take a look at Diesling's Patterns of Discovery in Social Science, where you will find a discussion of the criticism of non-traditional research methods and some suggestions on how these denunciations may be overcome.

Holistic theories tend to be concatenated rather than hierarchical and are loosely linked to the whole.

Example: Two pre-school children, one from a low socio-economic family and the other from a high socio-economic family are studied to determine the patterns of educational development in each. Their artwork, play activities, interaction with peers, etc. are used to help the researcher make inferences about their cognitive, conative, and affective development.

Grounded Theory

This type of inquiry, also known as "Analytic Induction," is one of the most sophisticated and developed approaches to rigorous qualitative (non-numerical) research. This type of research has its roots in symbolic interactionism and philosophy, and is used in areas where there is little previous research or in familiar areas where a new viewpoint would be greatly valued. Each datum is compared to every other datum as it is collected. Data are usually collected by participant observation and formal semi-structured interview. Data are simultaneously being collected, organized, analyzed, and interpreted to form new theories.

Grounded theory is an inductive technique developed for health-related topics by Glaser and Strauss (1967). It emerged from the discipline of sociology. The term *grounded* means that the theory developed from the research is "grounded," or has its roots, in the data from which it was derived. Grounded theory is based on symbolic interaction theory. This theory holds many views in common with phenomenology.

George Herbert Mead (1934), a social psychologist, was a leader in the development of this theory. Symbolic interactionism explores how people define reality and how their beliefs are related to their actions. People through attaching meaning to situations create reality. Meaning is expressed by symbols such as words, religious objects, and clothing. These symbolic meanings are the basis for actions and interactions. Grounded theory is used most often in studying areas where there has been little previous research and in gaining new insight into previously researched areas. Hence, it becomes an inductive method of gaining knowledge.

The steps of grounded theory research occur simultaneously. The researcher will be observing, collecting data, organizing data, and forming theory from the data at the same time. An important methodological technique in grounded theory research is the constant comparative process in which every piece of data is compared with every other piece.

Interview, observation, records, or a combination of these methods may be used to collect data. Data collection usually results in large amounts of hand-written notes, typed interview transcripts, or video/audio taped conversations that contain multiple data to be sorted and analyzed. Coding and categorizing the data initiates this process. The outcome is a theory explaining the phenomenon under study. The research report presents the theory supported by examples from the data. The literature review and numerical results are not used in the report. The report tends to be narrative discussions of the study process and findings. Clements, Copeland, and Loftus (1990) carried out a grounded theory study which looked at how parents coped with difficult times when caring for a chronically ill child. They conducted audiotaped interviews of 30 families who used their clinic. The following is a brief statement of theory that came from their research.

"The family of a chronically ill child develops specific ways of coping in an attempt to meet the needs of all its members. If support is available, equilibrium is achieved. If needs increase dramatically or support changes there is a lack of equilibrium"

In grounded theory the researcher decides what data to collect next on the basis of an emerging theory. Proponents of grounded theory (Glaser and Strauss, 1967), believe that conjecture must be generated from data by a constant comparison method, that is, a series of "double back steps," until a pattern finally emerges.

Example: Pre-school children from low socio-economic families are interviewed to determine their concerns regarding education. Once this information is collected, the researcher then explores the areas delineated with similar groups of children to determine the extensiveness of these concerns.

Cutting Board:

(Ethnographic)

This type of study has its roots in anthropology and seeks to develop an understanding of the cultural meanings people use to organize and interpret their experiences. This can be done through an "emic" approach (studying behaviors from within a culture) or through an "etic" approach (studying behaviors from outside the culture and examining similarities and differences across cultures). Data are usually obtained through participant observation by the researcher or research assistant, and then verified with the group living the phenomenon. Ethnography focuses on the culture of a group of people.

Ethnographic researchers can study broadly defined cultures (e.g., Californians, incarcerated teens) in what is sometimes referred to as a macro-ethnography. Alternatively, it may focus on more narrowly defined ones (e.g., the culture of the homeless in San Francisco, online mathematics teachers in traditional universities), referred to as micro-ethnography. An underlying assumption of the ethnographer is that every human group eventually evolves a culture that guides the members' view of the world and the way they structure their experiences.

The aim of the ethnographer is to learn from (rather than to study) members of a cultural group—to understand their worldview as they define it. Ethnographic researchers sometimes refer to emic and etic perspectives. An emic perspective refers to the way the members of the culture envision their world—it is the insider's view. The etic perspective, by contrast, is the outsider's interpretation of the experiences of that culture.

Ethnographers strive to acquire an emic perspective of a culture under study. Moreover, they strive to reveal what has been referred to as *tacit knowledge*: information about the culture that is so deeply embedded in cultural experiences that members do not talk about it or may not even be consciously aware of it.

Ethnographers almost invariably undertake extensive fieldwork to learn about the cultural group in which they are interested. Ethnographic research is typically a labor-intensive endeavor that requires long periods of time in the field—months and even years of fieldwork may be required. In most cases, the researcher strives to actively participate in cultural events and activities. The study of a culture requires a certain level of intimacy with members of the cultural group, and such intimacy can only be developed over time and by working directly with those members as an active participant. The concept of researcher as instrument is frequently used by anthropologists to describe the significant role the ethnographer plays in analyzing and interpreting a culture.

The steps of ethnographic research include: identifying the culture to be studied, conducting a thorough literature review, identifying the significant variables within the culture, gaining entrance into the culture, immersing oneself in the culture, acquiring informants, gathering data, analyzing data, describing the culture, developing theory.

Data collection involves primarily observation and interview. The researcher may become a participant/observer in the culture during the course of the study. Analysis involves identifying the meanings attributed to objects and events by members of the culture. These meanings are often validated by members of the culture before finalizing the results.

Example: High school students from low socio-economic families video-tape different types of educational institutions that they have attended; determine, from their perspective, the most pressing problems within these institutions; and make recommendations as to how these problems might best be remedied.

Cutting Board:

Delphi

This involves a series of questionnaires, each one being more structured and requiring more focus by the respondent than the preceding one. Delphi technique is used when the problem does not lend itself to precise analytical techniques, but can benefit from subjective judgments on a collective basis.

Delphi is primarily used in two modes: exploratory (to find out what's "out there"); or refinement (using "expert judgments" anonymously elicited to fine-tune quantitatively-oriented estimates). For the technique to work, the respondents' estimates need to be calibrated for over/under estimation errors; the questions need to be neutrally phrased; and some technique or researcher oversight is necessary to control for the inclusion of mutually exclusive data components in the Delphi analysis. This technique is gaining more popularity as members of listservs feed back information and perhaps try to come to a consensus on future directives. The Delphi method was originally developed at the RAND Corporation by Olaf Helmer and Norman Dalkey.

The Delphi method consists of a series of repeated interrogations, usually by means of questionnaires, of a group of individuals whose opinions or judgments are of interest. After the initial interrogation of each individual, each subsequent interrogation is accompanied by information regarding the preceding round of replies, usually presented anonymously. The individual is thus encouraged to reconsider and, if appropriate, to change his previous reply in light of the replies of other members of the group. After several rounds, the group position could be determined by averaging.

You can sometimes obtain names and addresses of experts who live far away and would be difficult to interview by using a "snowball sample" where you ask an expert in the field for a list of other experts in the field. To consult such experts, you may resort to a questionnaire instead of an interview. If you wish to question several persons simultaneously, you may consider using the Delphi method.

As it is difficult to make summaries of other than quantitative responses, the questions that are used in the Delphi process are usually quantitative, e.g., "What will the price of crude oil be in 20 years?" On the basis of the responses to this type of question, the researcher will be able to calculate means and ranges, among other things. One advantage of the method is that you can readily use the range as a measure of the reliability of the forecast. Of course, nothing prevents using qualitative or any other type of questioning if the nature of the object so requires.

If the respondents are amenable to the extra effort, they may be asked to justify their opinions, especially if they differ from that of the majority. The Delphi procedure is normally repeated until the respondents are no longer willing to adjust their responses.

Example: A researcher directs identical questions to a group of experts, asking them to give their opinions on how the future of the Internet might affect the future of education. In the next step, the researcher makes a summary of all the replies received, sends this to the respondents, and asks if any experts want to revise their original responses.

Cutting Board:

Quantitative and Qualitative Research

Quantitative research is "a formal, objective, systematic process in which numerical data are utilized to obtain information about the world" (Burns and Grove cited by Cormack, 1991, p. 140). Therefore, objectivity, deductiveness, generalizability, and numbers are features often associated with quantitative research. When researchers select their approach to a study it should be a reflection of which approach is most suitable for the topic under consideration. However it is also reasonable to suggest that it also reflects the bias of the researcher. The majority of medical research is quantitative (and considered to produce "hard," generalizable results) while much of research in the social sciences is qualitative (and considered to produce "soft" results).

In general, qualitative methodologies favor the view that the world is holistic, and that there is not a single reality. It further supports the view that reality, which is based on perceptions, is different for each person, changes over time, and derives meaning primarily from context. Below find some differences between qualitative and quantitative epistemologies.

Scientific discipline or rigor is valued because it is associated with the worth of research outcomes and studies are critiqued as a means of judging rigor. Qualitative research methods have been criticized for lack of rigor. However, these criticisms have occurred because of attempts to judge the rigor of qualitative studies using rules developed to judge quantitative studies. Rigor needs to be defined differently for qualitative research since the desired outcome is different (Burns, 1989; Dzurec, 1989; Morse, 1989; Sandelowski, 1986).

In quantitative research rigor is reflected in narrowness, conciseness, and objectivity and leads to rigid adherence to research designs and precise statistical analysis. Rigor in qualitative research is associated with openness, scrupulous adherence to a philosophical perspective, and thoroughness in collecting data, and consideration of all the data in the development of a theory. In order to be rigorous in conducting qualitative research the researcher must be willing to let go of certain long-held beliefs that have become unshakeable, although they might be mistaken, such as standardized tests are reliable and valid. This process is often referred to as deconstructing knowledge. The qualitative researcher will often seek to form new ideas (reconstructing) while continuing to recognize that the present paradigms exist.

Both designs, quantitative and qualitative, are said to be systematic. In fact having a system or following a process is a defining principle of research. Broadly speaking, quantitative research is thought to be objective whereas qualitative research often involves a subjective element. It is thought that in gaining, analyzing, and interpreting quantitative data, the researcher can remain detached and objective. Often this is not possible with qualitative research where the researcher may actually be involved in the situation of the research.

If the Department of Motor Vehicles wished to conduct a study on waiting times, a quantitative approach could be to measure how long people wait, and can be purely objective. However if the researcher was wanting to discover how the customers felt about their waiting time, they would have to come into contact with the customers and make judgments about the way they answered questions. If researchers asked: "How are you feeling, having waited an hour to get your license processed?" they would almost certainly register the customers' nonverbal behavior as well as document the responses; in this way the researchers are adding a subjective element to the study.

Quantitative research is inclined to be deductive. In other words it *tests theory*. This is in contrast to most qualitative research, which tends to be inductive. In other words it *generates theory*. Quantitative designs of research tend to produce results that can be generalized, whereas qualitative studies tend to produce results that are less easy to generalize. This has to do with the problem of the sample used at the time. We all know, for example, that our feelings about waiting can change dependent on our particular set of circumstances. Even if researchers encountered the same group of customers on another day, they might find different results. Generally, it is difficult to generalize with qualitative results. The major difference between quantitative research and qualitative research is that quantitative research uses data that are structured in the form of numbers or that can be immediately transported into numbers.

If the data cannot be structured in the form of numbers, they are considered qualitative. (Note that qualitative data can sometimes be handled in such a way as to produce quantitative data, e.g., the researcher exploring feelings of customers can analyze the responses in clusters that are negative or positive so as to produce a figure/percentage of negative-patient and positive-patient feelings and data can be analyzed using programs such as QSR NUD*ST.

QUALITATIVE	QUANTITATIVE
Theory development	Theory testing
Naturalistic or organic settings	Synthetic settings
Subjective	Objective
Observations, interviews	Tests, surveys
Descriptive statistics	Descriptive and inferential statistics
Generates hypothetical propositions	Generates predictive relationships
Philosophical roots: Phenomenology	Philosophical roots: Positivism, empiricism
Goal: Understanding, description, generate hypothesis	Goal: Prediction, control, confirmation, test hypothesis

Some questions to answer in designing a qualitative study:

- Are the basic characteristics or assumptions of a qualitative study clearly stated?
- Will the reader have an understanding on how this qualitative study differs from a quantitative study?
- Is there information provided so that a reader will understand the origins of the qualitative design for this research study?
- Will the reader gain an understanding on how the experiences of the researcher shape his or her values and bias to the research?
- Is information provided on how the researcher will gain entry to research sites (if needed) and how approval will be obtained to collect data?
- Are the procedures for collecting data thoroughly and clearly discussed? Are reasons provided for the particular method of data collection?
- Are methods to code information set forth?
- Are the specific data analysis procedures identified against specific research designs, such as for ethnographic approaches, grounded theory, case studies, and phenomenology?
- Is it clear how information validity and reliability will be conducted (see verification of information in qualitative study)?
- Are definitions, delimitations (boundaries), and limitations (weaknesses) stated?
- Are the research outcomes presented in view of existing theory and literature? Is there contribution to the existing theory base? Are you developing altogether new theory?

Verification in a Qualitative Study

Validity and reliability must be addressed in a qualitative study. The accuracy, dependability, and credibility of the information depends on it. There are various ways to address validity and reliability, including triangulation of information among different sources, receiving feedback from informants, forming the unique interpretation of events, and others. The example provided by Creswell (1997) is an excellent example of a qualitative procedure. In the opening descriptions of the "Qualitative Research Paradigm," which has been taken from several authors (as quoted in Creswell, p.161) is found:

> *The intent of qualitative research is to understand a particular social situation, event, role, group, or interaction. It is largely an investigative process where the researcher gradually makes sense of a social phenomenon by contrasting, comparing, replicating, cataloguing, and classifying the object of study. . . . this entails immersion in the everyday life of the setting chosen for the study; the researcher enters the informants' world and through ongoing interaction seeks informants' perspectives and meanings.*

According to Guba and Lincoln (1989) criteria that are meaningful within an evaluative process include the following: credibility, persistent observation, member checks, and expert review.

Credibility is parallel to internal validity with the focus of establishing the match between the responses of the experts (e.g., teachers, administrators, and parents in an educational study) and those realities represented by the evaluator and designer of the instrument (the researcher and the research in this study).

Persistent observation (Lincoln & Guba, 1986, pp. 303–304) requires sufficient observation to enable the evaluator to identify those characteristics and elements in the situation that are most relevant to the issue being pursued, and to focus on the details.

A member check is the process of verifying information with the targeted group. It allows the stakeholder the chance to correct errors of fact or errors of interpretation.

Expert review is one of the primary evaluation strategies used in both formative (How can this program be improved?) and summative (What is the effectiveness and worth of this program?) evaluation. It is often a good idea to provide experts with some sort of instrument or guide to insure that they critique all of the important aspects of the program to be reviewed.

And the winner is . . .

Which research methodology best describes the way you plan to do your study? Why?
_____
Which methodology was the runner up? Why? _____
_____

Terrific! You have just taken another important step toward successfully completing your research project. Keep cooking! In the next cutting board you can demonstrate your scholarly literacy by matching the research term with its description. Check your answers and make sure you master the nuances of the ones that you missed.

Cutting Board:

A Test of Your Research Acumen

1. hermeneutics	A. A theory in the field of criticism in which all texts and works of art have a multiplicity of meanings.
2. postmodern	B. A philosophical movement founded by Edmund Husserl based on the relationship between a subject and the objects in his/her world.
3. ontology	C. The art and craft of interpretation which concerns itself with secret and hidden meanings in texts, music, and works of art.
4. phenomenology	D. Concerned with the nature of knowledge. In particular the methodology used to derive, elicit, and analyze data.
5. historical	E. A test, survey, or questionnaire used for data collection.
6. epistemology	F. A strong dislike of person, group or people or things. An attitude that does not require action or elaborate rationale.
7. qualitative	G. A philosophical view of seeking to understand what reality is or what reality consists of.
8. deconstruction	H. A study centered on culture. The purpose is to develop an understanding of the cultural meanings people use to organize and interpret their experiences.
9. case study	I. A type of study based on feedback with the hope of coming to some type of consensus.
10. ethnographic	J. A movement that suggests multiple interpretations of events and that all knowledge is subjective.
11. delphi	K. A set of interrelated constructs, definitions, and propositions that presents a systematic view of phenomena.
12. theory	L. Research focused on reliable and replicable data, mostly deductive in nature. Assumes that attributes can be expressed in measurable terms. Objective.
13. bias	M. Research focused on inductive discovery, tends to be exploratory, descriptive, process oriented and concerned with theory development.
14. instrument	N. A research method that aims to assess the meaning of events and to interpret what might otherwise be considered merely as the happenstance of blind fortune.
15. quantitative	O. An intensive description and analysis of a particular social unit that seeks to uncover the interplay of significant factors that are characteristic of a unit.

Ans: 1-C, 2-J, 3-G, 4-B, 5-N, 6-D, 7-M, 8-A, 9-O, 10-H, 11-I, 12-K, 13-F, 14-E, 15-L

Be Aware of Health Hazards [Ethics of Research]

1 c. Responsibility

1 c. Competence

1 c. Moral and Legal Issues

1 c. Proper Representation

Now that you have selected a research topic and have placed it into a particular category, you are in an excellent position to digest research ethics.

The dictionary defines ethics as "moral principles or rules of conduct." Morals are defined as "that concerning right and wrong." Research ethics are, therefore, the rules of right and wrong concerning research. Since research almost always involves people it is important that your research does not affect people in a negative way.

Research inherently contains many paradoxes. As a researcher you need freedom to investigate, that is find out as much information as possible about the population you are studying, while adhering to an individual's "right to privacy." Ethical principles have been established to balance these issues.

1 c. Responsibility

"The researcher must have a fantastic love of truth."

Flaws and Fallacies in Statistical Thinking—Stephen Campbell

It is the responsibility of the researcher to have integrity, that is, truthfulness and honesty, when carrying out the project. Deliberately changing or inventing research results to suit your own ideas is viewed as an anathema in research.

In traditional scientific research, objectivity is the key word. Traditional research is based on facts and figures, not on personal opinions and biases. The researcher is not to affect or influence the subjects' opinions.

It is important, regardless of the type of research that you are doing, that you respect the culture and customs of the people you are studying and be rid of any cultural biases when carrying out and reporting research.

For Your Information and Education

The following is a summary of the Code of Ethics of the American Sociological Association.

1. Researchers must maintain scientific objectivity.

2. Researchers must recognize the limitations of their competence and not attempt to engage in research beyond such competence.

3. Every person is entitled to the right of privacy and dignity of treatment.

4. All research should avoid causing personal harm to subjects used in research.

5. Confidential information provided by a research subject must be held in strict confidentiality by the researcher.

6. Research findings should be presented honestly, without distortion.

7. The researcher must not use the prerogative of a researcher to obtain information for other than professional purposes.

8. The researcher must acknowledge all assistance, collaboration of others, or sources which information was borrowed from others.

9. The researcher must acknowledge financial support in the research report or any personal relationship of the researcher with the sponsor that may conceivably affect the research findings.

10. The researcher must not accept any favors, grants, or other means of assistance that would violate any of the ethical principles set forth above.

Statistical Truths and Fallacies

> *"Statistics are like bikinis. What they reveal is suggestive, but what they conceal is vital."*

Aaron Levenstein

You have an obligation, as a researcher, to use statistics responsibly. An awareness of statistical fallacies and deceptions can serve as a guide for "what not to do" in reporting information and help you become a more critical reviewer of other research that you study. Some common statistical fallacies to be aware of are:

Spurious Accuracy: The story is told about a man who, when asked the age of a certain river, replied that it was 3,000,004 years old. When asked how he arrived at this conclusion he claimed that when he first started coming to this river he was told it was 3,000,000 years old and that was exactly four years ago. This is an example of spurious accuracy. Many things can simply not be measured with as much accuracy as some purveyors wish to pretend.

Faulty Comparisons: In 1960 commercials for Hollywood Bread claimed it had fewer calories per slice than any other bread. The FTC maintained that the only reason a slice of Hollywood bread contained fewer calories was that is was more thinly sliced. The comparison was based on unequal units. Whenever two or more things are being compared with respect to one characteristic, it is necessary that important characteristics (dependent variables) are kept as similar as possible. (It is unethical, while comparing apples and oranges, to give the reader the impression that what is being compared are two apples.)

Accommodating Averages: There are many kinds of averages. From a formal statistical standpoint, some are more common then others. The average that most people relate to is the (arithmetic) mean/average which is a measure of central tendency obtained by adding all entries and dividing by the number of entries.

The median average is the number in the middle when all the entries are listed in order (if there are an even number of entries, then the median is the arithmetic mean of the middle two, the $n/2$ entry and the $n/2 + 1$ entry). The median is easy to compute, takes into account all the data, but is not sensitive to the magnitude of the data. (For example, it doesn't care if the last number was 0 or -34.)

The mode average is the term that occurs the most often. Although it is usually the easiest figure to obtain, it is only sensitive to the most common occurrence and thus does not take into consideration all the numbers.

Less frequently used "averages" are the harmonic mean (used to average different rates, e.g., if you traveled at 50 mph for 2 hours and 60 mph for 3 hours then you would have traveled a total of 280 miles in 5 hours at an average of 56 miles for the entire trip), and the geometric mean (used to average rates of growth).

A manager of a baseball team might find the median or mode average more advantageous than the mean average when negotiating salaries with players. The players, on the other hand, may prefer to use the arithmetic mean salary so that the salaries of the players who are making astronomical amounts would be considered and weighted into the determination of their wages.

The arithmetic mean average, although it is sensitive to all the data, does not, by itself, give us a picture of how the data is dispersed. To accomplish this the standard deviation, or the variance which is the standard deviation squared, should be reported. The variance is found by taking the difference between each entry and the mean, squaring these differences, and obtaining the (arithmetic) mean of the squared differences. To obtain the standard deviation all you, or your calculator, need do is take the square root of the variance.

If the standard deviation is relatively large compared to the mean, a wide dispersion of numbers is indicated. Conversely, a small standard deviation indicates that the numbers are clustered around the mean. Thus, it is generally expected that researchers report the mean and standard deviation when presenting findings.

The following is an empirical rule (68,95,99) that applies to data having a distribution that is approximately bell shaped:

About 68% of all scores fall within one standard deviation of the mean. About 95% of all scores fall within two standard deviations of the mean. About 99% of all scores fall within three standard deviations of the mean.

For example, the mean I.Q. on the Stanford-Binet test is 100 and the standard deviation is 15. Thus, 68% of those who have taken the test have I.Q.s between 85 and 115. This is often referred to as "normal." I.Q.s between 115 and 130 are considered "above average," those with I.Q.s between 130 and 145 are considered "genius," and those above 145 are classified as "brilliant."

Normally Distributed I.Q.s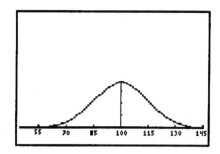

Ad Hoc Definitions: Whenever a term can be defined in more than one way, you must decide which of the possible definitions seems most sensible and which definition lends itself best to efficient data collection. (It is also important that you clearly define all concepts in your study which might be unfamiliar to your reader.)

A classic case of the need for a proper definition was found in 1955 when the population of London was reported in three different studies as:

5,200   **325,000**   **8,315,000**

whereas New York City was reported (in three different studies) to have a population of:

1,910,000   **10,350,000**   **8,050,000**

What became clear from these accounts is how meaningless a comparison between the populations of these cities (or any city) is without clearly defining geographic boundaries.

Rubber Graphs: The human eye has difficulty assimilating raw data or columns of numbers. Graphs often aid in making information more easily understood. A line graph is customarily used to note trends or compare amounts. The vertical axis generally has the measures (quantities) represented. The scales that are used will affect the appearance of the graph and should not be used to deceive people.

The Murky Notion of Cause and Effect: The story is told about a man who wrote a letter to an airline requesting that their pilots cease turning on the little light that says "FASTEN SEAT BELTS," because every time that light went on, the ride got bumpy. Be aware that in all correlational studies, effects may be wrongly attributed to factors that were merely "casually" associated rather than cause-and-effect related.

1 c. Competence

You should be properly qualified to carry out your research project. You should look at the problem you plan to study critically, then as objectively as possible judge your own abilities to devise procedures appropriate for examining the problem.

A competent researcher possesses certain personal qualities such as creativity, flexibility, curiosity, determination, objectivity, tolerance of frustration, logical reasoning abilities, and the ability to make scholarly observations. (Having come this far in your *Dissertation Cookbook,* you have already demonstrated many of these qualities.)

1 c. Moral and Legal Issues

The legal and social rules of the community you are investigating should be respected. If you think your work could break either the legal or social rules of the community, your research efforts should be curtailed until these issues are resolved.

Subjects often need to be assured that all personal information given to the researcher will be seen only by those who are carrying out the research project. It is unethical to discuss a person, or the information he or she gives you in confidence, with your family or friends. There is one exception to the confidentiality rule—legal obligation. If someone tells you about a serious legal offense or crime, you may have to break the confidentiality rule and notify the proper authorities.

Most research reports on groups of people keep the identity of individuals anonymous. When reporting anecdotal cases, identities can be hidden by the use of a false name or initials.

When you interview or test people you should explain to them the following:

1. Who will see the information they give,
2. What will be done with the information, and
3. How their privacy will be protected.

It is important for you, the researcher, to be viewed as a person concerned about the people being studied. You should not leave confidential questionnaires, papers, or interview notes lying around so that anyone can read them. It is best to keep these somewhere safe or, if possible, locked away so that they don't fall into the wrong hands.

Plagiarism

In conducting research, we are continually engaged with other people's ideas: we read them in texts, hear them in lectures we attend, share ideas on e-mail, discuss them with others, and incorporate them into our own writing. As a result, it is very important that we give credit where it is due. Plagiarism is using others' ideas and words without clearly acknowledging the source of that information.

To avoid plagiarism, you must give credit whenever you use:

- another person's idea, opinion, or theory;
- any facts, statistics, graphs, drawings—any pieces of information—that are not common knowledge;
- quotations of another person's actual spoken or written words; or
- paraphrase of another person's spoken or written words.

These guidelines are taken from the Student Code of Rights, Responsibilities, and Conduct found at Indiana Universities web page: *http://www.indiana.edu/~wts/wts/plagiarism.html*

Wth the advent of the World Wide Web and the proliferation of Distance Learning institutions, there is a limitless reservoir of digital documents that can be downloaded, studied, and—in some cases, unfortunately—plagiarized. If plagiarism is suspected the Web can also be used to search for the original source. Pasting key, specific phrases into a search engine like *www.yahoo.com* or *www.google.com* will often lead to the original source. In addition, there are Web sites that can run a plagiarism check and find documents with contents that match or are similar to the contents in a research paper. One such site that does not charge a fee is *www.findsame.com*. Another method to check for plagiarism is to look at the document in Word or Excel and check File > Properties to see who originally drafted the document and when. Other sites used to combat plagiarism are *http://scout.cs.wisc.edu, http://www.findsame.com/,* and *http://twist.lib.uiowa.edu/resources/ plagiarism.html.* Glatt company at *http://www.plagiarism.com/* provides software that helps "detect and deter" plagiarism. There is a student tutorial which provides computer assisted instruction on what constitutes plagiarism and how to avoid it. This includes definitions of direct and indirect plagiarism, when and how to provide attribution, and mastery test of concepts. This software is typically used in academic institutions or in the legal profession for cases of copyright infringement.

Internal Review Boards (IRBs): Ethical Issues Related to Conducting Research Using Human Subjects

There is a code of ethical standards to be adhered to in order to provide protection for all stakeholders involved in research. Even the best-intentioned research projects can provoke concerns about protecting the human subjects involved. To address these issues most institutions and organizations have created an Institutional Review Board (IRB). The IRB is a panel of people who review proposals and examine the ethical implications. They decide whether additional action should be taken to protect the rights of participants and guarantee their safety.

Ethical protections for participants of research include several elements but the major area of concern is the protection of human subjects. Voluntary participation in the research ensures that the subjects have not been forced to participate or are not held captive to the study. Additionally, participants must give informed consent in order to participate. These standards evolved from the previous use of human subjects without their consent and, often, without choice. People being held in prisons, universities, or hospitals were used as test subjects without their knowledge or consent.

There have been recent ethical concerns surrounding a participant's right to service when the research conducted uses an experimental group and a control group. The control group does not receive the treatment being researched. If the treatment is perceived to be beneficial to those receiving it, those in the control group may claim their right to equal access to benefits may be violated. For more information on this, and other important ethical issues, check out the following site: *http://www.orst.edu/instruct/coun510/ethics/educat.htm*

1 c. Proper Representation

Misrepresentation should not occur. When you carry out research you may find you have a powerful position and high status. You should not claim to have more qualifications than you actually have.

Researchers are responsible for protecting the welfare and dignity of the people they are researching. You must have informed consent from all subjects taking part. If people do not want to continue, they must have the right to withdraw without any repercussions.

In human research it is unethical (and often impossible) to arrange for negative conditions such as poor teaching, abusive parenting, alcoholism, etc.; however, the *consequences* of such conditions can be studied.

Warning: In this age of information, sponsored studies have become America's most powerful and popular tool of persuasion. Although the studies and surveys wear the guise of objective science, their findings almost invariably reflect their sponsors' intentions. Most such research is designed with a certain outcome in mind, and it is all but guaranteed to achieve that outcome. The result is a corruption of information—the information used every day by voters, consumers, and leaders. "Studies have become the vehicle for polishing corporate images, influencing juries, shaping debate on public policy, selling commercial products and satisfying the media's—and the public's—voracious appetite for information." In The Tainted Truth (1995) Cynthia Crossen details popular studies, which succinctly illustrate this grave situation.

What Can Be Done?

It is idealistic to believe that academic institutions, researchers, pollsters, or the media will universally decide to stifle their self-interest and clean up the information industry. One of the unfortunate results of our obsession with numbers and information is that we allow them to supersede our eyes, our judgment, and our common sense. Many people are afraid to try to pull apart statistics because they were "not good in math." What follows are things to think about while evaluating the veracity of OPR (other people's research):

1.   A little skepticism goes a long way: Does this make sense? Does it seem right?
2.   Unless and until a study has been replicated it should be looked at with care.
3.   Beware of "independent" researchers. This means they have many paying clients instead of one.
4.   Beware of "nonprofit" researchers. They still count on a regular salary.
5.   Beware of phrases like "as many as." This indicates hyperbole.
6.   What kind of reputation does the researcher enjoy as a supplier of the information or as an authority on the subject?
7.   Does the investigator have an "ax to grind"?
8.   What supportive evidence is offered?
9.   Some basic questions:
     a.   How many people were involved?
     b.   Over what period of time?
     c.   How was the study controlled for bias?
     d.   What did earlier studies find?
     e.   How were results presented?
     f.   Was the research peer-reviewed?
     g.   What kind of reputation does the source enjoy as a supplier of this type of information?
     h.   Is the source an authority on the subject?
     i.   What supportive evidence is offered?
     j.   Do estimates appear plausible?

Ultimately, the job of cleaning up the research business is everyone's responsibility.

Choose Your Attire [Form and Style]

When you attend a formal dinner, you are often advised on what the dress code will be: white tie, black tie, casual attire, etc. The same can be said for the serving or presenting of your feast (final dissertation copy): A certain form and style should be adhered to.

The assembling of your final manuscript usually requires adherence to a certain form and style with respect to each of the following aspects:

Pagination, footnotes, abbreviations, tables, illustrations, bibliography, references, quotations, layouts, capitalization, underlining, graphs, indenting, table of contents, acknowledgments, title page, chapter headings, parentheses, spacing, table of tables, and hyphenations.

Shortly after you start writing the preliminary draft of your research paper, it would be an excellent idea for you to determine what will be the format of your paper. The most important rule to follow is that of consistency, i.e., once you have determined that you will be using a certain style and form of writing, continue to use that exact style and form throughout your manuscript.

You should obtain a manual that aids writers in your discipline with respect to form and style. Such manuals exist for the biological sciences, engineering, humanities, law, mathematics, physical science, and psychology. It would also be helpful for you to scrutinize an approved dissertation from a colleague or classmate in your field with respect to the form and style they used or examine a dissertation in your field that is currently living in a university library.

The American Psychological Association (APA) manual is the most commonly used style and form guide in the social and behavioral sciences. An excellent resource can be found at *http://www.apa.org/journals/faq.html*

Below are some examples of how to reference books used as references in your research document according to APA guidelines.

One author: Nathan, A.J. (1990). *China's crisis: Dilemmas of reform and prospects for democracy.* New York: Columbia University Press.

Two authors: Simon, M., & Francis, B. (1997). *The dissertation cookbook.* Dubuque, IA: Kendall/Hunt.

Three authors: Linn, M., Fabricant, S., & Linn, D. (1988). *Healing the eight stages of life.* New York: Paulist Press.

More than three authors: Sakakibara, S., Hidetoshi, Y., Hisakatsu, S., Kengo, S., & Shimon, F. (1988). *The Japanese stock market: Pricing systems and accounting information.* New York: Praeger.

No author: *Diseases.* (1983). Springhouse, PA: Nursing 84 Books.

Corporate author: American Hospital Association. (1988). *American hospital association guide to the health care field.* Chicago: Author.

Editor: Adams, M. (Ed.). (1987). *The Middle East handbook.* New York: Facts on File.

Another quick guide can be found at: http://www.wooster.edu/psychology/apa-crib.htm#top

Phase 2
Accoutrements

Utensils [Instruments]
Serving Platters/Spices [Statistics]
Assistant Chefs [Population and Sample]

Utensils [Choosing Your Instruments]

What Will You Utilize to Gather Data?

Tests, Inventories, Questionnaires, Interviews, Observations: In Phase 2 of *The Dissertation and Research Cookbook* you will acquire proper utensils for the creation and serving of your feast. In addition, during this phase you will be forming the "bulk" of your main course, which you will ultimately complete in Phase 3.

Pre-Packaged Tests and Inventories (Just Stir and Serve)

Pre-Packaged tests and inventories are among the most useful tools for the chef/researcher. They have been seen at many eloquent banquets in the past. The benefits of using pre-packaged and standardized tests are that the items and total scores have been carefully analyzed and their validity and reliability have most likely been established by careful statistical controls.

Most pre-packaged tests have norms that are based upon the performance of many subjects of various ages living in many different types of communities and geographic areas. Among those to choose from are:

1. Achievement tests, which attempt to measure what an individual has learned. Achievement tests are designed to quantify an individual's level of performance based on information that has been deliberately taught. Most tests used in schools are achievement tests. They are used to determine individual or group status in academic learning, strengths and weaknesses defined by the test preparer, and as a basis for awarding prizes, scholarships, or degrees.

2. Aptitude tests, which attempt to predict the degree of achievement that may be expected from individuals in a particular activity. They are similar to achievement tests in their measuring of past learning, but differ in their attempt to measure non-deliberate or unplanned learning. They are often used to divide students into relatively homogeneous groups for instructional purposes, identify students for scholarship grants, screen for educational programs, and purportedly to predict future success.

3. Personality tests or inventories used by participants to report their own personality traits or tendencies. However, because of many people's inability or unwillingness to report their own actions accurately and objectively, their tendency to withhold embarrassing responses, and their unwillingness to express those qualities that are socially unacceptable, the effectiveness and the value of such tests are limited.
4. Psychological tests and inventories are instruments designed to describe and measure certain aspects of human behavior.

To determine if a pre-packaged test would be right for you, it would be an excellent idea to do an in-depth analysis of each question on each test that purports to measure a variable (characteristic) that you are examining. It is your responsibility to provide evidence that the examination selected is the most appropriate for the purpose at hand.

One of the best sources to help you select standardized tests is the Mental Measurements Yearbooks, edited by Oscar Buros and published by Gryphon Press. These yearbooks contain critical evaluations of tests and provide information concerning costs, availability of alternate forms, administration time required, names of subtests, grade or age levels for which tests were designed, and the name of publisher. It is, however, necessary to know the approximate year in which the exam was published to determine in which yearbook any particular exam was reviewed.

Cutting Board:

1. If you are planning to use a pre-packaged test or survey, write the name of the test and its reliability and validity information in the space below: _____
   _____
2. List the questions that you feel this test will answer with respect to some variable or characteristic you wish to measure in your study._____
   _____

Questionnaires or Surveys (Making Your Meal from Scratch)

Questionnaires or surveys are perhaps the most frequently used instruments for gathering data on population variables. Their appeal rests in their ability to get to the heart of the research under investigation.

The questionnaire often attempts to gather background characteristics such as age, education, gender, etc., and to elicit the feelings, beliefs, experiences, or activities of the respondents. It is used to help policy makers, program planners, evaluators, and researchers when information needs to come directly from the people.

Good questionnaires maximize the relationship between the answers recorded and the variable that the researcher is trying to measure. The answer is valuable to the extent that it can be shown to have a predictable relationship to facts or subjective states that are of interest.

One means of assuring that the questions are germane to the study is for the researcher to prepare a working table containing a list of questions related to the hypothesis under investigation. You will be given that opportunity in the cutting board activity provided in this section.

A consideration that needs to be made is what type of data will you obtain. There are four types of data that you can obtain. A mnemonic device used to remember these types of data is found in the French word for black, NOIR (nominal, ordinal, interval, ratio). Nominal and ordinal data are considered nonparametric data (non-numerical), whereas interval and ratio are considered parametric (numerical) data.

1. Nominal (name only) data are characterized by information that consists of names, labels, or categories only. This type of data cannot be arranged in an ordering scheme and is considered to be the lowest level of measurement. There is no criterion by which values can be identified as greater than or less than other values. We cannot, for example, average 12 democrats and 15 republicans and come up with 13.5 independents. We can, however, determine ratios and percentages and compare the results to other groups.

2. Ordinal (or ranked) levels of measurement generate data that may be arranged in some order, but differences between data values either cannot be determined or are meaningless. For example, we can classify income as low, middle, or high to provide information about relative comparisons, but the degrees of differences are not available.

3. Interval level of measurement is similar to the ordinal level, with the additional property that you can determine meaningful amounts of differences between data. This level, however, often lacks an inherent starting point. For example, in comparing the annual mean temperatures of states, the value of "0 degrees" does not indicate no heat and it would be incorrect to say that 40 degrees is half as warm as 80 degrees.
   Note: A special form of interval level measurement is the binary (or dummy) variable of 1,0. This code represents the presence (1) or absence (0) of a certain characteristic.

4. The ratio level of measurement is considered the highest level. It includes an inherent zero starting point and fractional values. As the name implies, ratios are meaningful for this type of measurement. The heights of children, distances traveled, and the amount of gasoline consumed, are ratio levels of measurement.

A general and important guideline to follow is that statistics based upon one level of measurement should not be used for a lower level. Implications made from interval and rational data can usually be determined by using parametric methods, whereas implications from ordinal and nominal data require the use of less sensitive nonparametric methods.

Another decision that you need to make is whether to use open-ended or closed-end questions. The advantages to open questions are:

1. You will be able to obtain answers that were unanticipated.
2. They tend to describe more closely the real views of the respondent.
3. Respondents will be able to answer questions in their own words.

However, closed questions are usually an easier way of creating data because:

1. The respondent can perform more reliably the task of answering the question when response alternatives are given.
2. The researcher can perform more reliably the task of interpreting the meaning of answers when the alternatives are given to the respondent.
3. They provide respondents with a constrained number of categories, increasing the likelihood that there will be enough people in any given category to be analytically interesting.
4. There is a strong belief that respondents find closed questions to be less threatening than open questions.

Cutting Board:

If you are planning to create a questionnaire, fill out the information below:

1. List four demographic questions you feel would be helpful to know about your sample.
2. What questions are you seeking answers to in your study?
3. List four other broad questions that you would like to obtain from your sample.
4. a. Underline the type of measurements you will most likely use:
       Nominal (name only, certain trait)
       Ordinal (a ranking system; Likert scale)
       Interval (fixed differences, but no fixed zero—temperature)
       Ratio (interval with a fixed zero—height, time, weight)
    b. Underline the type of questions you will most likely be asking:
       Open (subjects fill in the blanks)
       Closed (multiple choice)
5. What is the population you are studying?
6. Will you be sending the questionnaire to the whole population or to a subset (sample) of the population?
7. Will the survey be administered cross-sectional (just once) or longitudinal (over time)?
8. How will the survey be administered? Through the mail? Personal interview? Group setting?
9. Approximately how many questions do you plan to have?
10. Will you need permission and/or help to administer the questionnaire or obtain a mailing list? If yes, how will you obtain this assistance?

The following suggestions can help you to eliminate some obstacles that questionnaire designers often encounter. As you prepare your questions, check to see that each question you create adheres to the warnings given.

____ 1. When writing closed-end questions, it is an excellent idea to use Standard English.
____ 2. Keep the questions concrete and close to respondents' experience.
____ 3. Be aware of words, names, and views that might automatically bias results.
____ 4. Use a single thought per question.
____ 5. Use short questions and ask for short responses if possible.
____ 6. Avoid words that may be unfamiliar to the respondent.
____ 7. Define any word whose meaning might be vague.

_____ 8. Avoid questions with double negatives, such as: "This class is not the worst math class I have ever taken."
_____ 9. When using multiple choice questions, make sure all possibilities are covered.
_____10. Be as specific as possible.
_____11. Avoid questions with two or more parts.
_____12. Give points of reference as comparisons, e.g., instead of asking, "Do you like mathematics?" you might ask:

Please rank your favorite academic classes from most favorite (1), to least favorite (4):

Social Studies _____ English _____ Science _____ Mathematics_____
_____13. Underline or use bold print for words that are critical to the meaning of the questions, especially negative words like **not.**
_____14. Ask only important questions since most respondents dislike long questionnaires or questionnaires that ask too many unimportant questions.
_____15. Avoid suggestive questions or questions that contain biases. "Would you support more money in mathematics education if the schools continue to use the same outdated teaching methods?" reflects the researcher's bias on mathematics education.
_____16. When asking questions regarding ethnic background or political affiliations, use alphabetical order.

In addition, the following receive high honors in the culinary research arts:
_____17. Be efficient and brief. A questionnaire should only be as long as necessary.
_____18. Be objective. The test should be as objective as the situation dictates.
_____19. Be interesting. The questionnaire should be as interesting and as enjoyable as possible.
_____20. Be simple. The questionnaire should be simple to administer, score, and interpret.
_____21. Be clear. It is important that the directions be clear so that each participant can understand exactly the manner in which the test is to be taken.

A widely used type of ordinal measurement on closed questionnaires is the Likert-type scale, named after its creator. The original Likert scale used five categories: strongly approve, approve, undecided, disapprove, and strongly disapprove.

In a Likert-type scale, points are assigned to each of the categories being used. The most favorable response is usually given the most points, that is, favorableness of the attitude, not the response category itself. A Likert-type scale may use fewer or more than five categories. In general, the more categories there are, the better the reliability.

The placement of items should be randomized. Placing all of the favorably worded items first may produce a set or tendency for respondents (e.g., the subjects might fill in all fives without reading the questions).

The score that the individual receives on a Likert-type scale is the sum of the scores received on each item. For example, if 25 items are on a questionnaire and each item contains a minimum of one point and a maximum of five points, then the highest possible score would be 125, whereas the lowest possible score would be 25 (assuming no items were missing).

Once you have custom-designed your questionnaire or test, you will need to consider the instrument's reliability and validity. Reliability is concerned with the accuracy (consistency, stability, and repeatability) of a measure in representing the true score of the subject being assessed on a particular dimension. The same results must be achieved, as far as possible, regardless of who is doing the measuring. Reliability of measurement reduces influence or bias on the part of the person(s) doing the measurement to a minimum.

Reliability provides an estimate of how well measurements reflect true (non-random) differences. There are three main types of reliability coefficients that can be measured:

1. Stability. The extent to which individuals maintain their relative standings when the same or similar exam is administered twice over a period of time.
2. Equivalence. Correlation of scores on two or more forms of the same test by the same persons.
3. Internal consistency. Correlation between questions on the same test to determine if they measure the same trait.

As a researcher, you are obligated to select the most reliable instruments. The purpose of the testing determines, in part, the minimum reliability coefficient that can be tolerated. However, reliable tests may not necessarily be valid tests.

Validity refers to the extent to which measurements achieve the purpose for which they are designed. The researcher needs to determine the validity of the content.

Some questions that could determine whether or not a test is valid are:

1. Does each item measure predetermined criteria?
2. Do previously obtained scores accurately predict the criteria measured?
3. Does the behavior or conditions of administrating the test affect the results?

When you report your findings from your survey or questionnaire you will need to include:

1. The population you took the sample from.
2. How the people were contacted.
3. The number contacted, the number responding, and the response rate.
4. Any evidence that the people who responded are a representative, unbiased sample of the population.
5. How the survey was distributed.
6. The date the survey was conducted.

7. Any caveats the reader should keep in mind as they interpret the findings. These might include cautions about a low response rate, a response group that is not quite representative of the overall population, or anything that has happened since the survey was conducted that might affect results were it repeated today.

Cutting Board:

This would be an excellent time to create your questionnaire. Insert a separate sheet of paper and compose your questionnaire now. Check to see that you have incorporated the ideas suggested in this section. Enjoy the challenge!

Adjuncts to Questionnaires

Pilot Study
Cover Letter
Going the Extra Mile

Pilot Study

Before the final form of the questionnaire is constructed, it is useful to conduct a pilot study to determine if the items are yielding the kind of information that is needed. Check to see if there is any ambiguity, or if the respondents have any difficulty in responding. Administering the questionnaire personally and individually to a small group of respondents is usually the way to proceed with your pilot study.

The pilot instrument should invite comments about the perceived relevance of each question to the stated intent of the research. It would also be beneficial to provide a means for the respondent to suggest additional questions that the researcher did not include.

Cover Letter

If questionnaires are administered to an intact group such as students in a class or members of a congregation, then you will have the opportunity to inform the respondents of the intent of the study and motivate them to complete the questionnaire. However, when questionnaires are sent through the mail, it may be difficult to motivate respondents to fill out the questionnaire and to return it within a reasonable period of time. Unless the potential respondents believe that the questionnaire is of value, it is likely that they will become non-respondents. For this purpose, a cover letter usually accompanies the questionnaire.

If a recognized group or a prestigious organization sponsors the research, this information should be stated in the cover letter, since such information often adds credibility to the study.

The cover letter should also state that:

1. The questionnaire will not take a great deal of time to complete.
2. Each individual's personal attention to the questionnaire is of extreme importance to the study.

In addition, the following ingredients enhance the efficacy of the cover letter:

3. An introduction: The name of the researcher and the company, organization, or university that is requesting or approving this study.
4. A purpose: The reason for conducting the study, the use for this questionnaire, and its value to the investigation should be explained. The sole intention of a study should not be that a student expects to obtain a degree by means that include the use of this questionnaire (however important that is). It is unlikely that a potential respondent would take the time to carefully fill out a questionnaire for this goal.

    Note: You must also be careful not to reveal too much. This might bias the study and make the results invalid.
5. A list of directions: Explain how the questions are to be answered, how the questionnaire is to be returned, and if there is some reasonable deadline for returning it. Indicate whether or not the respondent needs to put his or her name on the form, and any other relevant information that should be included with the questionnaire.
6. Return postage: It is unreasonable to ask the respondent to provide postage for the questionnaire's return.

The researcher should avoid the use of "obvious" form letters or letters where the initial salutation is:

Dear _____, or "To Whom It May Concern."

You should also sign the letter personally.

Extra attention and a personal touch demonstrate the sincerity of the research effort and the importance of the respondents' participation.

Note: Without your taking the aforementioned information into consideration, it is likely that the questionnaire will only make it to the nearest trash receptacle.

Cutting Board:

This would be an excellent time to create your cover letter. Insert a separate sheet of paper and compose your cover letter NOW! Check to see that you have incorporated the ideas suggested in this section.

Going the Extra Mile

Some ways to encourage respondents to perform the task of filling out the questionnaire, especially if the questionnaire is mailed, are:

1. Make personal contact by phone or in person, prior to sending out the questionnaire.
2. Offer some type of financial compensation or gift. (For short questionnaires, some companies put a questionnaire on the back of a small check.)
3. Make the cover letter and questionnaire attractive looking.
4. Make the cover letter personal.
5. Make repeated contact with non-respondents.

A reasonable sequence of events may be:

1. About 10 days after the initial mailing, mail all non-respondents a reminder card emphasizing the importance of the study and the need for a high response rate.
2. About 10 days after the postcard is mailed, mail the remaining non-respondents a letter again emphasizing the importance of a high rate of return and including another questionnaire for those who threw the first one away.
3. If the response rate is still not satisfactory, it would be advisable to call non-respondents on the telephone or send a telegram or e-mail.

The difficulties of getting the response rate to a reasonable level will depend on the nature of the sample, the nature of the study, the motivation of the people who are to complete the questionnaire, and the ease with which the questionnaire may be completed.

Cutting Board:

If you are planning to mail out questionnaires, which of the methods above do you think you will employ to increase the response rate? _____

The Personal Interview

The personal interview has many similarities to the questionnaire. The major advantages of using an interview instead of a questionnaire are:

1. The response rate is generally high.
2. It is an especially useful technique when dealing with children or an illiterate population.
3. It eliminates the misinterpretation of a question.
4. The subject is more likely to have any misunderstandings clarified.
5. It can encourage a relaxed conversation where questions can be asked in any order depending on the response of the interviewee.
6. It provides an opportunity to find out what people really think and believe about a certain topic through questioning.
7. It is more flexible and allows the interviewer to follow "leads" during the interview.
8. The interviewer can interpret body language as an extra source of information.

Note: A good interviewer has HEARTS: Honesty, Earnestness, Adaptability, Reliability, Trustworthiness, and Sincerity.

Some disadvantages of the interview method are:

1. Time and economy. Questionnaires can usually be sent through the mail; thus, for the price of postage and printing, the questionnaire can reach practically anyone under consideration. Furthermore, the expense and time involved in training interviewers and sending them to interview respondents needs to be considered.

2. Reliability of information can be questioned because of interviewer bias.
3. Difficulties often arise in quantifying or statistically analyzing data obtained from interviews.

All surveys obtained through questionnaires or interviews adhere to the same ethical system: The privacy of the individual is respected and weighed against the public's right to know.

For Your Information and Education

The results of surveys that deal with sensitive issues are felt by many to be dubious. People are often not willing to reveal private details about their lives.

However, there is a statistical method that can allow investigators to ask questions in a way that is likely to elicit honest responses. Stanley Warner developed this method in 1965. It completely protects the privacy of individuals yet provides good survey information. It is called randomized response.

Suppose question ten on a survey is: "Have you used illegal drugs in the past week?" The respondent is told to read the question and flip a coin. He/she is to answer "NO" only if the coin comes up tails and they have not used illegal drugs. Otherwise, they should answer "YES." The proportion of the group that would have answered "NO" is then computed to be twice those that actually responded NO (the other half got heads), e.g., if 40% wrote NO then 80% of the sample is determined to have not used illegal drugs in the past week. People have commented that they trust this method in maintaining their privacy and are more willing to answer these questions honestly.

Cutting Board:

1. If you are planning to use the personal interview, list the reasons for your decision.
2. Who will do the interviewing? Why?

Observation

Obtaining data through observation, both participant and non-participant, is becoming more and more common. It is perhaps the most direct means of finding out information, especially if your study is focused on deeds rather than words. The extent of your personal involvement depends on which of the two methods you choose.

In non-participant observation:

1. Your presence may be known or unknown.
2. You may observe through a device such as a one-way glass, or may rely on observations from video or audio taping.
3. The data obtained tend to be fairly subjective.

The major advantage to using participant observation is that you can experience firsthand the psychological and social conditions that produce different decisions and practices.

The disadvantages to using participant observation are:

1. You could be influenced by your own interpretation and personal experiences.
2. Questions of reliability exist, since others may interpret an experience differently than you.
3. Your presence might affect the subject and the situation being observed.

One way to reduce these disadvantages is to read your report to the people observed and to ask for comments, additions, or deletions prior to its formalization.

Accuracy is the key to making this type of data collection effective. Special training is needed to move from casual observer to systematic observer. In using structured observation techniques, the researcher usually searches for a relationship between independent variables to a dependent variable. The researcher must thus be able to code and recode data in a meaningful way and be aware of the potential biases he/she brings to research.

For Your Information and Education

All methods of data collection have advantages and disadvantages compared to other methods. The method you choose should be based upon the aims and objectives of the study and the population being studied. However, when you write your research paper you should include the advantages and disadvantages of the instrument you chose, and explain how you attempted to minimize the disadvantages.

Serving Platters/Spices [Statistics]

Featuring: What's Stat? (You Say?)
How to Exhibit Your Date (a)

What's Stat? (You Say?)

Statistics is like trying to determine how many different colored m&m's are in a king size bag by looking at only a carefully selected handful.

The job of a statistician involves: C O A I P

1/2 c.	"C"ollecting
1/2 c.	"O"rganizing
1 c.	"A"nalyzing
1-2 c.	"I"nterpreting
1 c.	"P"redicting

Statistics can be used to predict, but it is very important to understand that these predictions are not certainties. The fact that conclusions may be incorrect separates statistics from most other branches of mathematics. If a fair coin is tossed ten times and ten heads appear, the non-statistician would incorrectly report that the coin is biased. This conclusion, however, is not certain. It is only a "likely conclusion," reflecting the very low probability of getting ten heads in ten tosses.

After data are collected, they are used to produce various statistical numbers such as means, standard deviations, percentages, etc. These descriptive numbers summarize or describe the important characteristics of a known set of data. In hypothesis testing, descriptive numbers are standardized so that they can be compared to fixed values (found in tables or in computer programs) that indicate how "unusual" it is to obtain the data you collected. Once data are standardized and significance determined, you may be able to make inferences about an entire population (universe).

Note: Your *The Dissertation and Research Cookbook* intends to give you a substantial "taste" of statistics so that you will feel comfortable with this aspect of your "feast" preparation. You have already "nibbled" on statistics in the last section when you explored different methods of "collecting" data.

You might wish to seek further "condiments" to add to the knowledge you will acquire from your *Dissertation Cookbook* or consult with a statistician after reading the information in Phase 2 to help you decide which statistics, if any, would be applicable to your study. You are encouraged to use statistical programs or business calculators to perform the hackneyed computations that often arise during statistical testing. Remember: You are ultimately responsible for the results. You must be aware of why you are using a certain test, know what assumptions are made when such a test is used, understand what the test results indicate, and understand how this analysis fits in with your study.

The Role of Statistics

Statistics is merely a tool. It is not the be-all and end-all for the researcher. Those who insist that research is not research unless it is statistical display a myopic view of the research process. These are often the same folks who are equally adamant that unless research is "experimental research" it is not research.

One cardinal rule applies: The nature of the data governs the method that is appropriate to interpret the data and the tool of research that is required to process those data. A historian seeking to answer problems associated with the assassination of Dr. Martin Luther King, Jr., would be hard put to produce either a statistical or an experimental study, and yet the research of the historian can be quite as scholarly and scientifically respectable as that of any quantitative or experimental study.

Statistics many times describes a quasi-world rather than the real world. You might find that the mean grade for a class is 82 but not one student actually received a grade of 82. Consider the person that found out that the average family has 1.75 children and with heartfelt gratitude exclaimed: "Boy, am I grateful that I was the first born!" What is accepted statistically is sometimes meaningless empirically. However statistics is a useful mechanism and a means of panning precious simplicity from the sea of complexity. It is a tool that can be applied to practically every discipline!

Frequently Asked Questions (FAQ's) about Statistics

1. What is the purpose of statistics? The purpose of statistics is to collect, organize, and analyze data (from a sample), interpret the results and try to make predictions (about a population). We "do" statistics whenever we COAIP—collect, organize, analyze, interpret, and predict—data. One relies on statistics to determine "how close" to what one anticipated would happen actually did happen.
2. Why and how would one use inferential statistics? In inferential statistics we compare a numerical result to a number that is reflective of a chance happening, and determine how significant the difference between these two numbers is.
3. Are predictions indisputable in statistics? Statistics can be used to predict, but these predictions are not certainties. Statistics offers us a "best guess." The fact that conclusions may be incorrect separates statistics from most other branches of mathematics. As mentioned above, if a fair coin is tossed ten times and ten heads appear, the non-statistician would incorrectly report that the coin is biased.
4. What are hypotheses? Hypotheses are educated guesses (definitive statements) that are derived by logical analysis using induction or deduction from one's knowledge of the problem and from the purpose for conducting a study. They can range from very general statements to highly specific ones. Most research studies focus on the proving or the disproving of hypotheses.

Broad Area	Hypothesis (or Hypotheses for the Plural)
Employee Motivation	The implementation of an attendance bonus is positively related with employee attendance.
	There is a positive relationship between providing employees specific sales goals and their obtaining these goals.
Employee Satisfaction	There is a positive relationship between employee satisfaction and participatory management style.
	There is a positive relationship between employee satisfaction and the frequency of communication management delivers to employees.
Marketing	Implementation of the QED teller system has significantly improved customer satisfaction with ABC Bank.
	Customers have a significantly higher preference for the XYZ Bank's location in a grocery store to traditional bank locations.
Quality	The customer satisfaction is higher in Company A than in Company B.

5. What is statistical hypothesis testing? Statistical hypothesis testing, or tests of significance, is used to determine if the differences between two or more descriptive statistics (such as a mean, percent, proportion, standard deviation, etc.) are statistically significant or more likely due to chance variations. It is a method of testing claims made about populations by using a sample (subset) from that population.

   In hypothesis testing, descriptive numbers are standardized so that they can be compared to fixed values, which are found in tables and in computer programs, which indicate how "unusual" it is to obtain the data collected. A statistical hypothesis to be tested is always written as a null hypothesis (no change). Generally the null hypothesis will contain the symbol "=" to indicate the status quo, or no change. An appropriate test will tell us to either reject the null hypothesis or fail to reject (accept) the null hypothesis. Check out: *http://math.uc.edu/~brycw/classes/148/tables.htm* to find out how to test a computed value against a critical value.

6. Once I find a test that helps to test my hypothesis is there anything else I need to be concerned about? Certain conditions are necessary prior to initiating a statistical test. One important condition is the distribution of the data. Once data are standardized and the significance level determined, a statistical test can be performed to analyze the data and possibly make inferences about an entire population (universe).

7. What are "*p*" values? A *p*-value (or probability value) is the probability of getting a value of the sample test statistics that is at least as extreme as the one found from the sample data, assuming the null hypothesis is true. Traditionally, statisticians used "alpha" values that set up a dichotomy: reject/fail to reject conclusion. *P*-values measure how confident we are in rejecting a null hypothesis. If a *p*-value is less than 0.01 we say this is "highly statistically significant" and there is very strong evidence against the null hypothesis. *P*-values between 0.01 and 0.05 indicate that it is statistically significant and adequate evidence against the null hypothesis. For *p*-values greater than 0.05, there is, generally, insufficient evidence against the null hypothesis.

8. What is data mining? Data mining is an analytic process designed to explore large amounts of data in search of consistent patterns and/or systematic relationships between variables, and then to validate these findings by applying the detected patterns to new subsets of data. There are three basic stages in data mining: exploration, model building or identifying patterns, and validation and verification. If the nature of available data allows, it is typically repeated until a "vigorous" model is identified. However, in business decision making, options to validate the model are often limited. Thus, the initial results often have the status of general recommendations or guides based on statistical evidence (e.g., soccer moms appear to be more likely to drive a mini-van than an SUV).

9. What are the different levels of measurement? Data come in four types and four levels of measurement, which can be remembered by the French word for black: **NOIR**—Nominal (lowest), Ordinal, Interval, and Ratio

Nominal Scale	Measures in terms of name of designations or discrete units or categories. *Example:* Gender, color of home, religion, type of business.
Ordinal Scale	Measures in terms of such values as more or less, larger or smaller, but without specifying the size of the intervals. *Example:* rating scales, ranking scales, Likert-type scales.
Interval Scale	Measures in terms of equal intervals or degrees of difference but without a zero point. Ratios do not apply. *Example:* Temperature, GPA.

| Ratio Scale | Measures in terms of equal intervals and an absolute zero point of origin. Ratios apply. *Example:* Height, delay time, weight. |

A general and important guideline is that the statistics based on one level of measurement should not be used for a lower level, but can be used for a higher level. An implication of this guideline is that data obtained from using a Likert-type scale (a scale in which people set their preferences from, say, 1 = totally agree to 10 = totally disagree) should generally not be used in parametric tests. The good news is that there is almost always an alternative approach using nonparametric methods.

10. What types of distribution can be found when data are collected? One of the most important characteristics related to the shape of a distribution is whether the distribution is skewed or symmetrical. Skewness (the degree of asymmetry) is important. A large degree of skewness causes the mean to be less acceptable and useful as the measure of central tendency. To use many parametric statistical tests requires a normal (symmetrical) distribution of the data. Graphical methods such as histograms are very helpful in identifying skewness in a distribution. Check out *http://www.stat.sc.edu/webstat/*.

If the mean, median, and mode are identical, then the shape of the distribution will be unimodal, symmetric, and resemble a normal distribution. A distribution that is skewed to the right and unimodal will have a long right tail, whereas a distribution that is skewed to the left and unimodal will have a long left tail. A unimodal distribution that is skewed has its mean, median, and mode occur at different values. For highly skewed distributions, the median is the preferred measure of central tendency, since a mean can be greatly affected by a few extreme values on one end.

Kurtosis is a parameter that describes whether the particular distribution concentrates its probability in a central peak or in the tails. (How "pointed" or flat" a distribution looks.) Normal populations lie at 3 on this scale, non-normal populations lie on either side of 3.

11. What is the difference between a parametric and a nonparametric test? Most of the better-known statistical tests use parametric methods. These methods generally require strict restrictions such as:
1. The data should be ratio or interval.
2. The sample data must come from a normally distributed population.
Good things about nonparametric methods:
1. Can be applied to a wider variety of situations and are distribution free.
2. Can be used with nominal and ranked data.
3. Can use simpler computations and be easier to understand.
Not so good things about nonparametric methods:
1. Tend to waste information since most of the information is reduced to qualitative form.
2. Generally less sensitive, so stronger evidence is needed to show significance—that could mean larger samples are needed.
Checkout: http://www.seeingstatistics.com

How to Exhibit Your Date (a)

Data which are collected but not organized are often referred to as "raw" data. It is common to seek a means by which the human mind can easily assimilate and summarize "raw" data. Frequency tables and graphs delectably fulfill this purpose.

For Your Information and Education

A frequency table is so named because it lists categories of scores along with their corresponding frequencies. This is an extremely simple and effective means of organizing data for further evaluation. For a large collection of scores, it might be best to use a statistical program such as Statview, SPSS, or GBSTAT, where you enter the raw data into your computer and then with the mere press of a button or two, construct an awesome frequency table.

If the data you obtained are demographic (about personal characteristics or geographical regions) then it would be beneficial to present the percentages of these characteristics within the sample (e.g., 24% of the subjects studied were Hispanic). If you determine an arithmetic mean in your study, then both the mean and the standard deviation should be presented.

Data are often represented in pictorial form by means of a graph. Some common types of graphs include pie charts (if you are picturing the relationship of parts to a whole), histograms

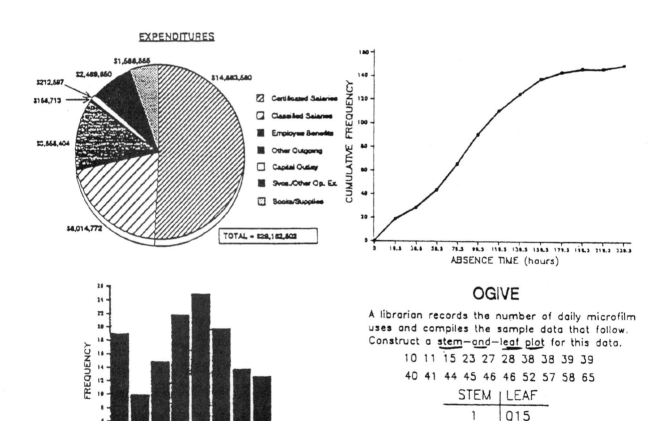

OGIVE

A librarian records the number of daily microfilm uses and compiles the sample data that follow. Construct a <u>stem-and-leaf plot</u> for this data.

10 11 15 23 27 28 38 38 39 39

40 41 44 45 46 46 52 57 58 65

STEM	LEAF
1	015
2	378
3	8899
4	014566
5	278
6	5

(if you are displaying the different types of numerical responses with respect to the frequency in which they occur. A histogram is similar to a bar graph, which is often used to represent the frequency of nominal data), ogives (if you are displaying cumulative frequencies such as incomes under $10,000), or stem and leaf plots (if you wish the actual data to be preserved and used to form a picture of the distribution).

Note: Statistical computer programs, like SPSS and STATVIEW, can instantaneously produce frequency tables; compute means, percentages, and standard deviations; and generate suitable graphs reflecting your findings once you have appropriately input raw data. (They never complain about doing any of these things.) By a click of a mouse you can order a statistical test and in under a second know whether to accept or fail to accept your statistical hypothesis!

Check out http: www.stat.sc.edu/webstat/ http://www.faculty.vassar.edu/~lowry/webtext.html

---

Cutting Board:

1. Arrange your data in a frequency table. (If you have administered a questionnaire, you might wish to list the different responses to each question in conjunction with the frequency with which they were selected.)
2. Construct appropriate graphs to picture the distributions determined by your frequency table.
3. Compute any statistical numbers that are descriptive of your data such as means, standard deviations, proportions, per cents, quartiles, etc. (You may wish to use a calculator or a computer that is programmed to determine your mean and standard deviation, with the mere press of a button, once information has been entered in a befitting manner. The manual that comes with the machine or computer program could prove helpful for this task.)

Definitions

One of the keys to understanding a specialized field is getting to know its jargon—its technical vocabulary. As you continue to put together your research project you might come across words that you are unfamiliar with. The following words often appear in quantitative studies.

Alternative Hypothesis: The hypothesis that would be accepted if the null hypothesis is not accepted.

Analysis of Variance (ANOVA): A statistical method for determining the significance of the differences among a set of sample means.

Central Limit Theorem: A mathematical conjecture that informs us that the sampling distribution of the mean approaches a normal curve as the sample size, N, gets larger.

Chi-square Distribution: A continuous probability distribution that could be used to test hypotheses involving variation.

Confidence Interval: A range of values used to estimate some population parameter with a specific level of confidence. In most statistical tests, confidence levels are between 95% and 99%.

Correlation: A relationship between variables such that increases or decreases in the value of one variable tend to be accompanied by increases or decreases in the other.

Correlation Coefficient: A measurement between −1 and 1 indicating the strength of the relationship between two variables.

Critical Region: The area of the sampling distribution that covers the value of the test statistics that are not due to chance variation. In most tests it represents between 1% and 5% of the graph of the distribution.

Critical Value: The value from a sampling distribution, which separates chance variation to variation, that are not due to chance.

Data: Facts and figures collected through research. The word data is plural, just like the word "toys." Data are us. :)

Dependent Variable: The variable that is measured and analyzed in an experiment. In traditional algebraic equations of the form $y =$ _____ $x +$ _____, it is usually agreed that y is the dependent variable.

Dependent Samples: The values in one sample are related to the values in another sample. Before and after results are dependent samples.

Descriptive Statistics: The methods used to summarize the key characteristics of known population and sample data.

Degrees of Freedom: The number of values that are free to vary after certain restrictions have been imposed on all values.

Experiment: Process that allows observations to be made. In probability an experiment can be repeated over and over again under the same conditions.

***F* Distribution:** A continuous probability distribution used in tests comparing two variances.

Goodness of Fit: Degree to which observed data coincide with theoretical expectations.

Histogram: A graph of connected vertical rectangles representing the frequency distribution of a set of data.

Hypothesis: A statement or claim that some characteristic of a population is true.

Hypothesis Test: A method for testing claims made about populations. Also called test of significance. In this tutorial the CANDOALL method is used to test hypotheses.

Independent Variable: The treatment variable. In traditional algebraic equations of the forms $y =$ _____ $x +$ _____, it is usually agreed that x is the independent variable.

Inferential Statistics: The methods of using sample data to make generalizations or inferences about a population.

Interval Scale: A measurement scale in which equal differences between numbers stand for equal differences in the thing measured. The zero point is arbitrarily defined. Temperature is measured on an interval scale.

Kruskal-Wallis Test: A nonparametric hypothesis test used to compare three or more independent samples.

Left-tail Test: Hypothesis test in which the critical region is located in the extreme left area of the probability distribution. The alternative hypothesis is the claim that a quantity is less than a certain value.

Level of Significance: The probability level at which the null hypothesis is rejected. Usually represented by the Greek letter alpha (α).

Mean: A measure of central tendency, the arithmetic average; the sum of scores divided by the number of scores.

Median: A measure of central tendency which divides a distribution of scores into two equal halves so that half the scores are above the median and half are below it.

Mode: A measure of central tendency that represents the most fashionable, or most frequently occurring, score.

Multiple Regression: Study of linear relationships among three or more variables.

Nominal Data: Data that is names only, having no real quantitative value. Often numbers are arbitrarily assigned to nominal data, such as Male = 0, Female = 1.

Nonparametric Statistical Methods: Statistical methods that do not require a normal distribution or that data be interval or rational.

Normal Distribution (Gaussian Curve): A theoretical bell-shaped, symmetrical distribution based on frequency of occurrence of chance events.

Null Hypothesis: The null hypothesis is a hypothesis about a population parameter. It assumes "no change" or status quo (=). The purpose of hypothesis testing is to test the viability of the null hypothesis in the light of experimental data. Depending on the data, the null hypothesis either will or will not be rejected as a viable possibility.

Odds in Favor: The number of ways an event can happen compared to the number of ways that it cannot happen.

Ogive: A graphical method of representing cumulative frequencies.

One-tailed Test: A statistical test in which the critical region lies in one tail of the distribution.

One-way Analysis of Variance: Analysis of variance involving data classified into groups according to a single criterion.

Ordinal Scale: A rank-ordered scale of measurement in which equal differences between numbers do not represent equal differences between the things measured. The Likert-type scale is a common ordinal scale.

Parameter: Some numerical characteristic of a population.

Parametric Methods: Types of statistical procedures for testing hypotheses or estimating parameters based on population parameters that are measured on interval or rational scores. Data are usually normally distributed.

Pie Chart: Graphical method of representing data in the form of a circle containing wedges.

Population: All members of a specified group.

Probability: A measure of the likelihood that a given even will occur. Mathematical probabilities are expressed as numbers between 0 and 1.

Probability Distribution: Collection of values of a random variable along with their corresponding probabilities.

***P*-value:** The probability that a test statistic in a hypothesis test is at least as extreme as the one actually obtained. A *p*-value is found after a test statistic is determined. It indicates how likely it is that the result of an experiment was due to a chance happening.

Qualitative Variable: A variable that is often measured with nominal data.

Quantitative Variable: A variable that is measured with interval and rational data.

Random Sample: A subset of a population chosen in such away that any member of the population has an equal chance of being selected.

Range: The difference between the highest and lowest score.

Ratio Scale: A scale that has equal differences and equal ratios between values, and a true zero point. Heights, weights, and time are measured on rational scales.

Raw Score: A score, obtained in an experiment, which has not been organized or analyzed.

Regression Line: The line of best fit that runs through a scatterplot.

Right-tailed Test: Hypothesis test in which the critical region is located in the extreme right area of the probability distribution. The alternative hypothesis is the claim that a quantity is greater than a certain value.

Sample: A subset of a population.

Sampling Error: Errors resulting from the sampling process itself.

Scattergram: The points that result when a distribution of paired values are plotted on a graph.

Sign Test: A nonparametric hypothesis test used to compare samples from two populations.

Significance Level: The probability that serves as a cutoff between results attributed to chance happenings and results attributed to significant differences.

Skewed Distribution: An asymmetrical distribution.

Spearman's Rank Correlation Coefficient: Measure of the strength of the relationship between two variables.

Spearman's Rho: A correlation statistic for two sets of ranked data.

Standard Deviation: The "weighted" average amount that individual scores deviate from the mean of a distribution of scores. A measure of dispersion equal to the square root of the variance. At least 75% of all scores will fall within the interval from two standard deviations from the mean. At least 89% of all scores will fall within three standard deviations from the mean.

Standard Error of the Mean: The standard deviation of all possible sample means.

Standard Normal Distribution: A normal distribution with a mean of 0 and a standard deviation equal to one.

Statistic: A measured characteristic of a sample.

Statistics: The collection, organization, analysis, interpretation, and prediction of data.

***T* Distribution:** Theoretical, bell-shaped distribution used to determine significance of experimental results based on small samples. Also called the student *t* distribution.

***T*-test:** Significance test that uses the *t* distribution.

Test Statistic: Used in hypothesis testing, it is the sample statistic based on the sample data.

Two-tailed Test of Significance: Any statistical test in which the critical region is divided into the two tails of the distribution. The null hypothesis usually is that a variable is equal to a certain quantity.

Type I Error: The mistake of rejecting the null hypothesis when it is true.

Type II Error: The mistake of failing to reject the null hypothesis when it is false.

Uniform Distribution: A distribution of values evenly distributed over the range of possibilities.

Variance: The square of the standard deviation. A measure of dispersion.

Wilcoxon Rank-Sum Test: A nonparametric hypothesis test used to compare two independent samples.

***Z*-score:** A score expressed in standard deviation units used to compare the relative standing of scores in two distributions.

Assistant Chefs [Identifying Your Population and Choosing Your Sample]

Most chief chefs employ a variety of people to assist them in producing an eloquent banquet. Similarly, most researchers depend upon other people to help them obtain the information that they need to prepare their dissertation or research report.

If you are planning to conduct a survey or interview people, one major issue is to get *enough* people whose views count. Usually it is not practical or possible to study the entire universe or population, so you might need to settle for a sample or a subset of the universe. In choosing a sample and a method of data collection, you need to ask yourself certain questions:

1. How quickly are the data needed?
2. What are the resources available?
3. Should probability or non-probability sampling be used?

Things to consider when conducting a sample:

Data carelessly collected may be so completely useless that no amount of statistical torturing can salvage them—*garbage in, garbage out*! There are four points to consider when collecting data.

1. Ensure the sample size is large enough for the required purpose (this will be discussed in hypothesis testing).
2. When possible do the measuring yourself. Self-reporting tends to lead to political correctness, wishful thinking, or disproportionate rounding, and, therefore, distorted data.
3. How will data be collected? Mail surveys tend to get lower responses, and personal interviews are time consuming and expensive but may be needed for complete data. Telephone interviews are relatively efficient and relatively inexpensive.
4. Ensure that the sample is representative of the population.

The following are common means of sampling:

1. Random sampling (representative, proportionate). Members of the population are selected in such a way that each has an equal chance of being selected. This needs much planning to avoid haphazard sampling. Telephone directories, for example, leave out unlisted numbers. In Los Angeles 42.5% of telephone numbers are unlisted. Computer generated numbers are better. There is about a 20% refusal rate for telephone interviews, which could bias the study.
2. Stratified sampling. Members of the population are subdivided into at least two different sub-populations or strata, e.g., gender. Samples are then drawn from each stratum.
3. Systematic sampling. Similar to random sampling. Members of the population are listed in some type of roster and then every kth (e.g., 20th) element is chosen.
4. Cluster sampling. Members of the population are divided into sections (or clusters), randomly select a few of those sections and then choose all the members for the selected sections. For example, in conducting a pre-election poll we could randomly select 30 election precincts and survey all people from those precincts. The results may need to be adjusted to correct for any disproportionate representation of groups. Used extensively by government and private research organizations.
5. Snowball sampling. Another technique for finding research subjects. In this method, one subject gives the researcher the name of another subject, who in turn provides the name of a third, and so on. This is an especially useful technique when the researcher wants to survey or interview people with unusual characteristics who are likely to know one another.
6. Convenience sampling (non-probability sampling). Uses results that are readily available. Sometimes this is quite good—e.g., a teacher wanting to know about left-handed students' needs; sometimes it may be seriously biased.

Non-probability sampling is something we all use in everyday life. If you want to try out a new brand of crackers, you know that you only need to choose one cracker from one box to decide if you like the cracker because the others are expected to taste pretty much the same. Another common form of non-probability sampling may be carried out when trying to conduct "on the street" interviews. Researchers will often have some bias toward which people they will sample.

In convenience sampling one uses the results that are readily available. Sometimes this is quite good—e.g., a teacher wanting to know about left-handed students' needs would not include those who are right-handed. However, such sampling can be seriously biased when researchers choose only those they feel comfortable working with.

Sometimes non-probability sampling is done inadvertently. Back in 1933 a telephone poll indicated that Alf Landon would overwhelmingly become our next president. If you have difficulty remembering President Landon's record, your vexation is justified. What became obvious, after this study was analyzed, was that it failed to take into account that Republicans had most of the phones in 1933 and that Roosevelt's supporters were the majority without telephones.

If a non-probability survey is to be conducted, you must be very careful not to generalize too much from it. It is, however, very useful in the early stages of developing your study in order to get some new ideas and in the development of some interview questions, in practicing interviews and surveying techniques, or in a pilot study. At times, only a small sample of the population is available to participate in a study.

Non-probability samples are usually easier to obtain but the gains in efficiency are often matched with losses in accuracy and generality.

Sometimes thousands of people are sampled to get the data needed; on other occasions, a sample may be as small as one.

Some factors affecting the size of a sample are:

1. the size of the universe or population being studied,
2. the purpose of the study,
3. the potential application of the result of the study,
4. the type of statistical tests, and
5. the research techniques being used.

By having a relatively large sample you are usually able to see the general, overall pattern, but since in many tests the significance of measures is a function of sample size, it is possible to get a statistically significant relation when the strength of the relationship is too small to be used. Under sound statistical practices using simple random samples obtained through probability means, you can often get excellent information from a sample size of 30 or less.

Sometimes a case study of one or two subjects is the most appropriate means of conducting an investigation. This enables you to obtain detailed information about a problem in which there is much interest but little information.

Case studies are usually selected by non-probability sampling according to your judgment about whether the sample is a good representative of the population. For example, most information obtained about the (Idiot) Savant Syndrome has been obtained through individual case studies of these extraordinary people.

Linda Suskie, in her book *Questionnaire Survey Research: What Works* (1996), provides a guide to determine how many people you can survey based on sampling error. A sampling error of 5% means that you can be 95% sure that you have the correct statistics. The table below is from her book.

Random Sample Size	Sample Error
196	7%
264	6%
364	5%
1,067	4%
2,401	2%
9,604	1%

In most studies a 5% sampling error is acceptable. Below are the sample sizes you need from a given population.

Population Size	Sample Size
10,000	370
5,000	357
2,000	322
1,000	278
500	217
250	155
100	80

These numbers assume a 100% response rate.
Suskie, Linda. (1996). *Questionnaire Survey Research: What Works* (2nd Ed.). Washington, DC: Assn. for International Research.

The size of the survey may be decided with statistical precision. A major concern in choosing a sample size is that it should be large enough so that it will be representative of the population from which it comes and which you wish to make inferences about. It ought to be large enough so that important differences can be found in subgroups such as men and women, democrats and republicans, groups receiving treatment and control groups, etc.

Two major issues to be considered when using statistical methods to choose sample size are sampling error and confidence levels.

Sampling error: Some small differences will almost always exist among samples and between them and the population from which they are drawn. One approach to measuring sample error is to report the standard error of measurement, which is computed by dividing the population standard deviation (if known) by the square root of the sample size. Minimizing sampling error helps to maximize the sample's representativeness.

Example: If the Stanford-Binet IQ test (where standard deviation is 15) is administered to 100 subjects, then the standard error of the mean would be 15/10 or 1.5

Confidence levels: You will need to decide how confident you wish, or need, to be that your sample is representative of the population. Frequently, the 95% confidence level is chosen. This means that there is a 95% chance that the sample and the population will look alike and a 5% chance that they will not.

Note: We can use the following formula to determine the sample size necessary to discover the "true" mean value from a population.

$$n = \left[\frac{\bar{z}\, \sigma}{E} \right]^2$$

where $\bar{z}$ corresponds to a confidence level (found on a table or computer program). Some common $\bar{z}$ values are 1.645 or 1.96, which might reflect a 95% confidence level (depending on the statistical hypothesis under investigation), and 2.33, which could reflect a 99% confidence level in a one-tailed test and 2.575 for a two-tailed test where σ is the standard deviation, and E is the margin of error.

Example: If we need to be 99% confident that we are within 0.25 lbs. of a true mean weight of babies in an infant care facility, and s = 1.1, we would need to sample 129 babies:

n = [2.575 (1.1)/0.25]^2 = 128.3689 or 129.

Note: A formula that we can use to determine the sample size necessary to test a hypothesis involving percentages is:

$$n = \frac{[\bar{z}]^2}{E^2} pq$$

where n = sample size, $\bar{z}$ = standard score corresponding to a certain confidence level, p is an estimate of the population proportion, and $q = 1 - p$. We represent the proportion of sampling error by "E," and the estimated proportion or incidence of cases by "p."

Example: Suppose that studies conducted 2 years ago found that 18% of drivers talk on a cell phone while driving. We want to do a study to check if this percentage is still true. We want to estimate, with a margin of error of three percentage points, the percentage of drivers who talk while driving today. If we need to be 95% confident of our result, how many drivers would we need to survey?

$$n = \frac{[1.96]^2}{0.03^2} (.18)(.82) = 1068$$

Cutting Board:

1. What is the population and sample that you will be studying?_____
_____
2. How will you select your sample? Why?_____
3. What measures will you take to see that your sample size is adequate for your study?

How to (Ap)praise Your Date (a)

Statistical Hypothesis Testing

    1 c. Analyzing

    1 c. Interpreting

    1 c. Predicting

Featuring:

- Essential Steps in Hypothesis Testing $S^3 d^2 CANDOALL$
- How to Choose Desirable Spices (tests)
- Testing Claims about:
  - means
  - standard deviations
  - proportions
  - relations
- Non Parametric Tests

In this section we will be exploring Statistical Hypothesis Testing to determine how close to what you anticipated would happen, actually did happen. You might also wish to check out: *http://davidmlane.com/hyperstat/logic_hypothesis.html*

Hypotheses are educated guesses that are derived by logical analysis using induction or deduction from your knowledge of the problem and from your purpose for conducting the study. They can range from very general statements to highly specific ones. Most research studies focus on the proving or the disproving of hypotheses.

After the data have been collected and organized in some logical manner, such as a frequency table, and a descriptive statistic (mean, standard deviation, percentage, etc.) is computed, then a statistical test is often used to analyze the data, interpret what this analysis means in terms of the problem, and make predictions based on these interpretations.

You might wish to visit this section once before all your data is collected and then plan a re-visit once your data is known.

Note: When you use statistics you are comparing your numerical results to a number that is reflective of a chance happening and determining how significant the difference between these two numbers is.

If you are planning to use statistical hypothesis testing as part of your dissertation (research project), you should read this section slowly and carefully, paying close attention to key words and phrases. Make sure you are familiar with all the terminology employed.

Note: If your study involves quantitative data and the testing of hypotheses, you will undoubtedly find the examples in this part of *The Dissertation and Research Cookbook* extremely beneficial. It is our intent to familiarize you with the techniques of the statistician and help you determine which statistical tests would work best for your study. Remember to keep a positive mental attitude as well as an open and inquisitive mind as you digest the information in this section.

There is a myth that statistical analysis is a difficult process that requires an advanced degree. This need not be the case. Statistical Hypothesis Testing can be fun and easy.

Although many esoteric tests exist (just as there are many exotic spices in the universe) most researchers use mundane tests (the way most chefs prepare delicious meals with common spices). The mundane "spices" for statistical hypothesis testing are: z-tests, t-tests, chi-square tests, F-tests, and rho-tests.

As you carefully and cheerfully read through this section you will learn which of these "spices" might best compliment your meal. Just as in cooking, sometimes you will find more than one spice that could be apropos and could enhance your meal. In analyzing your data you will likely find more than one type of statistical test that would be appropriate for your study, and the choice is often yours to make.

Testing a Claim about a Mean

The example in this section will be testing a claim about a mean obtained from a sample. If you can answer yes to one or more of the questions below, you could use this identical statistical test in your study.

Are you claiming that:

____1.   A new product, program, or treatment is better than an existing one?
____2.   An existing product, program, or treatment is not what it professes to be?
____3.   A group is under (or over) achieving?

Note: The recipe in this section can be used to check any statistical hypothesis (not just a statistical hypothesis about a mean), so it would behoove you to read through the following example with eager anticipation and note any similarities between this study and your study.

Example: Ms. Rodriguez (Ms. R) has found a new method of teaching reading (NMTR) that she claims is better than traditional methods. The average seventh grader reads at a 7.5 reading level by mid-year. Ms. R claims that NMTR will increase the average reading level significantly by mid-year.

To test her claim, Ms. R samples 36 students (n = 36) who have been using NMTR and finds that by mid-year the mean average of this group is 7.8. However, since the standard deviation of the population is 0.76, this could indicate that the sample students are just within normal boundaries.

Statistical hypothesis testing will be used to determine if the sample mean score of 7.8 represents a statistically significant increase from the population mean of 7.5, or if the difference is more likely due to chance variation in reading scores.

Before the 8-step statistical test (CANDOALL) "recipe" is employed, you need to procure five preliminary pieces of information—three begin with the letter *s* and two with the letter *d*: s^3d^2

(s) What is the substantive hypothesis?

(What does the researcher think will happen, based on a sound theoretical framework?)

Ms. R claims that NMTR will significantly increase the average reading level of seventh grade students by mid-year.

Cutting Board:

Write one substantive hypothesis apropos your study, i.e., what do you think (claim) that your study will reveal? _____

(s) How large is the sample that was studied?

Ms. R sampled 36 seventh grade students (n = 36) who have been using NMTR

(s) What descriptive statistic was determined by the sample?

The mean average of the sample, $\bar{x}$, was 7.8

(d) What type of data were collected?

Ms. R used ratio data.

(If data were nominal or ordinal then a nonparametric test would be called for.)

(d) What type of distribution did the data form? Many parametric statistical tests require a normal distribution of the data. Graphical methods such as histograms are very helpful in identifying skewness in a distribution. If the statistic you are testing is a mean and the data type is ratio, then a *z*-test or *t*-test will likely be applied. These tests are pretty "robust" and can be applied even if the data are skewed.

Ms. R will not need to be concerned about the distribution of her data.

Cutting Board:

1. Determine the sample size for your study, n = _____.
2. What descriptive statistic was obtained from your study? _____
   (You may wish to give an approximate value or result that you think you might obtain from your study to practice applying this process.)

   _____

Now we are ready to take the information obtained by the three s's and two d's and employ an 8-step recipe to create a "delicious" statistical test.

We will determine if Ms. R's claim, "NMTR increases the reading level of seventh graders," is statistically correct.

1. Identify the claim **[C]** to be tested and express it in symbolic form. The claim is about the population and that is reflected by the Greek letter μ.

    $$\mu > 7.5$$

    That is, Ms. R claims that the mean reading score, μ, of the seventh grade students who could use NMTR is greater than the population mean, 7.5
    Write your claim in symbolic form.

2. Express in symbolic form the statement that would be true, alternative **[A]**, if the original claim is false. *All cases must be covered.*

    $$\mu \leq 7.5$$

    Write the opposite of your claim in symbolic form (remember to cover all possibilities).

---

3. Identify the null **[N]** and alternative hypothesis.
    Note: The null hypothesis should be the one that contains no change (an equal sign).
      H_0: $\mu \leq 7.5$ (Null hypothesis)
      H_1: $\mu > 7.5$ (Alternative hypothesis)
    Determine the null and alternative hypotheses in your study.
    Note: A statistical test is designed to accept or reject (a.k.a. faii to accept) the statistical null hypothesis being examined.

4. Decide **[D]** the level of significance, alpha α, based on the seriousness of a "type I error," which is the mistake of rejecting the null hypothesis when it is in fact true. Make alpha small if the consequences of rejecting a true alpha are severe. The smaller the alpha value, the less likely you will be to reject the null hypothesis. Alpha values 0.05 and 0.01 are very common. The default α is 0.05:

    $$\alpha = 0.05$$

For Your Information and Education

Some researchers do not use alpha values (which are pre-determined at the beginning of a statistical test and indicate acceptable levels of significance). Instead, they prefer *p*-values (which indicate actual levels of significance of a claim and leave the conclusion as to whether this is "significant enough" to the reader). It is possible to do both (set α and compute *p*) and then compare these two values when reporting the findings.

Before a test of hypotheses is employed we can be certain that only four possible things can happen. These are summarized in the table below.

		Claim is tested	
		H0	H1
Decision	H0	**Correct Acceptance**	Type II Error β
	H1	Type I Error α	**Correct Rejection**

Note that there are two kinds of error represented in the table. Many statistics textbooks present a point of view that is common in business decision making: α, the type I error, must be kept at or below 0.05, if at all possible,

β, the Type II error rate, must be kept low as well. "Statistical power," which is equal to $1 - \beta$, must be kept correspondingly high. Ideally, power should be at least .90 to detect a reasonable departure from the null hypothesis.

5. Order [O] a statistical test relevant to your study—see table 1. Since the claim involves a sample mean and $n > 30$ we can compute a z-value and use a z-test. A z-value is a number we compute which can be graphed as a point on the horizontal scale of the standard normal distribution (bell-shaped) curve. This point indicates how far from the population mean (expected mean under the null conditions) our sample mean is, and thus enables us to determine how "unusual" our research findings are.

For Your Information and Education

The Central Limit Theorem implies that for samples of sizes larger than 30 the sample means can be approximated reasonably well by a normal (z) distribution. The approximation gets better as the sample size, n, becomes larger.

When you compute a z value you are converting your mean to a mean of 0 and your standard deviation to a standard deviation of 1. This allows you to use the standard normal distribution curve and its corresponding table to determine the significance of your values regardless of the actual value of your mean or standard deviation.

A standard normal probability distribution is a bell-shaped curve (also called a Gaussian curve in honor of its discoverer, Karl Gauss) where the mean or middle value is 0, and the standard deviation, the place where the curve starts to bend, is equal to 1 on the right and −1 on the left. The area under every probability distribution curve is equal to 1 or 100%). Since a Gaussian curve is symmetric about the mean, it is important to note that the mean divides this curve into two equal areas of 50%. Approximately 68% of the data are within one standard deviation of the mean.

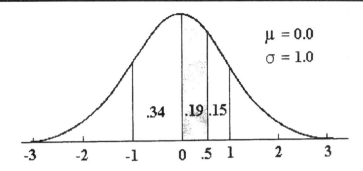

$\mu = 0.0$

$\sigma = 1.0$

.34 .19 .15

-3   -2   -1   0 .5 1   2   3

Blood cholesterol levels, heights of adult women, weights of 10-year-old boys, diameters of apples, scores on standardized test, etc., are all examples of collections of values whose frequency distributions resemble the Gaussian curve.

If you were to record all the possible outcomes from the toss of 100 different coins by graphing the number of heads that could occur on the horizontal axis (0,1,2,3 . . . 100), and the frequency with which each of the numbers of heads could occur on the vertical axis, you will produce a graph resembling the normal distribution. (The most "frequent" results would cluster around 50 heads and become less and less frequent as you consider values further and further from 50.)

6. Do the Arithmetic: [A] Determine the test statistic, the critical value; (s), and the critical region.

    The sample mean, $\bar{x}$, of 7.8 is equivalent to a z value of 2.37. This value is the test statistic, and was computed using the following formula:

$$z = \frac{\bar{x} - \mu}{\sigma / \sqrt{n}}$$

$\bar{x}$ = sample mean, μ = population mean, n = size of sample, σ = population standard deviation

    Thus, $z = (7.8 - 7.5)/(0.76)/6 = 2.37$ (to the nearest hundredth)

    Note: z numbers usually vary between −3 and +3. If they are outside of this range the null hypothesis will almost always be rejected (or an error was made).

    Note: $\sigma / \sqrt{n}$ (sigma divided by the square root of n) is often called the standard error of the mean or the standard deviation of the sample means.

    Note: Sometimes you can substitute the actual standard deviation of the sample, s, for the population standard deviation, s, if s is unknown.

    The $\alpha = 0.05$ level enables us to find a z value that will separate the curve into 2 unequal regions: the smaller one with an area of 0.05 (5%), and the larger one with an area of 100% − 5% or 95% (0.95). (Often referred to as a 95% confidence level.)

    Z values indicate the percent of area under the bell-shaped curve from the mean (middle) towards the "right tail" of the curve. Thus, for an alpha of 0.05, we need to determine what z value will cut off an area of 45% (0.4500) from the mean towards the "right tail." (We already know that 50% of the area is on the left side of the mean. We obtain 95% by adding 45% to 50%.)

Hunting through the vast array of four digit numerals in the table, we find our critical value to be between 1.6 (see z column) + .04 (1.64) that (reading down the .04 column) determines an area of .4495, and 1.6 + .05 (1.65), which determines an area of .4505. Thus, if we take the mean average of 1.64 and 1.65, we can blissfully determine the critical value to be 1.645, and the critical region to be all z values greater than 1.645. This determination requires us to reject the null hypothesis if our test statistics z value is greater than 1.645.

Note: Since there is only one alternative hypothesis, H1 μ > 7.5, we call this is a one-tailed (right-tailed) test. If our alternative hypothesis was $\mu \neq$ 7.5, a two-tailed test would be used since there would be two alternatives: μ < 7.5 or μ > 7.5.

An entry in the table is the proportion of the area under the entire standard normal curve, which is between z = 0 and a positive value of z. Areas for negative values are obtained by symmetry.

Z	0	0.01	0.02	0.03	0.04	0.05	0.06	0.07	0.08	0.09
0	0.00000	0.00399	0.00798	0.01197	0.01595	0.01994	0.02392	0.02790	0.03188	0.03586
0.1	0.03983	0.04380	0.04776	0.05172	0.05567	0.05962	0.06356	0.06749	0.07142	0.07535
0.2	0.07926	0.08317	0.08706	0.09095	0.09483	0.09871	0.10257	0.10642	0.11026	0.11409
0.3	0.11791	0.12172	0.12552	0.12930	0.13307	0.13683	0.14058	0.14431	0.14803	0.15173
0.4	0.15542	0.15910	0.16276	0.16640	0.17003	0.17364	0.17724	0.18082	0.18439	0.18793
0.5	0.19146	0.19497	0.19847	0.20194	0.20540	0.20884	0.21226	0.21566	0.21904	0.22240
0.6	0.22575	0.22907	0.23237	0.23565	0.23891	0.24215	0.24537	0.24857	0.25175	0.25490
0.7	0.25804	0.26115	0.26424	0.26730	0.27035	0.27337	0.27637	0.27935	0.28230	0.28524
0.8	0.28814	0.29103	0.29389	0.29673	0.29955	0.30234	0.30511	0.30785	0.31057	0.31327
0.9	0.31594	0.31859	0.32121	0.32381	0.32639	0.32894	0.33147	0.33398	0.33646	0.33891
1	0.34134	0.34375	0.34614	0.34849	0.35083	0.35314	0.35543	0.35769	0.35993	0.36214
1.1	0.36433	0.36650	0.36864	0.37076	0.37286	0.37493	0.37698	0.37900	0.38100	0.38298
1.2	0.38493	0.38686	0.38877	0.39065	0.39251	0.39435	0.39617	0.39796	0.39973	0.40147
1.3	0.40320	0.40490	0.40658	0.40824	0.40988	0.41149	0.41309	0.41466	0.41621	0.41774
1.4	0.41924	0.42073	0.42220	0.42364	0.42507	0.42647	0.42785	0.42922	0.43056	0.43189
1.5	0.43319	0.43448	0.43574	0.43699	0.43822	0.43943	0.44062	0.44179	0.44295	0.44408
1.6	0.44520	0.44630	0.44738	0.44845	**0.44950**	**0.45053**	0.45154	0.45254	0.45352	0.45449
1.7	0.45543	0.45637	0.45728	0.45818	0.45907	0.45994	0.46080	0.46164	0.46246	0.46327
1.8	0.46407	0.46485	0.46562	0.46638	0.46712	0.46784	0.46856	0.46926	0.46995	0.47062
1.9	0.47128	0.47193	0.47257	0.47320	0.47381	0.47441	0.47500	0.47558	0.47615	0.47670
2	0.47725	0.47778	0.47831	0.47882	0.47932	0.47982	0.48030	0.48077	0.48124	0.48169
2.1	0.48214	0.48257	0.48300	0.48341	0.48382	0.48422	0.48461	0.48500	0.48537	0.48574
2.2	0.48610	0.48645	0.48679	0.48713	0.48745	0.48778	0.48809	0.48840	0.48870	0.48899
2.3	0.48928	0.48956	0.48983	0.49010	0.49036	0.49061	0.49086	**0.49111**	0.49134	0.49158
2.4	0.49180	0.49202	0.49224	0.49245	0.49266	0.49286	0.49305	0.49324	0.49343	0.49361

Note: **The p-value** is .0089. We arrived at this value quite easily. Recall, in step 6, when we did the arithmetic, we computed the z-value between scores to be 2.37. If you go down the left side of the table and find a z value of 2.3, then go across to the .07 column, you will find the number .**4911**. This indicates an area of 49.11% from the mean z value of 0 to the z value of 2.37. Thus, 50% + 49.11% or 99.11% of the area of the curve is to the left of 2.37 and the small tail to the right of 2.37 has an area of 100% – 99.11% = 0.89% **or 0.0089,** which is our *p*-value.

   Note: Check out *http://math.uc.edu/~brycw/classes/148/tables.htm* to find out how you can test a computed value against a critical value.

7. Look **[L]** to reject the null hypothesis if the test statistic is in the critical region. Fail to reject the null hypothesis if the test statistic is not in the critical region.

   Ms. R's *z* value is in the critical region since 2.37 > 1.645. Thus we will reject the null hypothesis.

   For more on this test check out: http:duke.usak.ca/~rbaker/tables.html

---

Cutting Board:

---

8. Restate the previous decision in lay **[L]** or simple nontechnical terms.

We have reason to believe that NMTR improves the reading level of seventh grade students.

For Your Information and Education

If your sample size, *n*, is less than 30 and the population standard deviation is unknown, but there is a normal distribution in the population, then you can compute a "*t*" statistic

$$t = \frac{\bar{x} - \mu}{s / \sqrt{n}}$$

where *s* is the standard deviation of the sample, μ is the mean under contention, and *n* is the size of the sample.

Notice that *z* and *t* statistics are computed exactly the same way; the only difference is in their corresponding values of significance when you (or your computer) check these values on the graph or table.

In this example we tested a claim about a numerical value—mean test scores on a standardized test. The sample data came from a population which was known to have a normal distribution. We were thus able to use parametric methods in our hypothesis testing.

In general, when you test claims about interval or rational parameters (such as mean, standard deviation, or proportions), and some fairly strict requirements (such as the sample data has come from a normally distributed population) are met, you should be able to use parametric methods.

If you do not meet the necessary requirements for parametric methods, do not despair. It is very likely you will be able to use alternative techniques named, appropriately, nonparametric methods.

Since they do not require normally distributed populations, nonparametric tests are often called distribution-free tests. Some advantages to using nonparametric methods include:

1.   They can often be applied to nominal data that lack exact numerical values.
2.   They usually involve computations that are simpler than the corresponding parametric methods.
3.   They tend to be easier to understand.

Unfortunately, there are the following disadvantages:

1.   Nonparametric methods tend to "waste" information, since exact numerical data are often reduced to a qualitative form. Some treat all values as either positive (+) or negative (−). (A dieter using this test would count a loss of 50 lbs. as the same as a loss of 2 lbs.)
2.   They are generally less sensitive than the corresponding parametric methods. This means that you need stronger evidence before rejecting the null hypothesis, or larger sample sizes.

Cutting Board:

1.   My data are best described as:
      A.   Parametric (deal only with numbers that are integers or ratios)
      B.   Nonparametric (deal with ordered numbers, rankings, or names only)
2.   Checking Table 1, I find an appropriate statistical test(s) to check the validity of my hypothesis will be: _____

TABLE 1. Recommended Methods of Cooking—Hypothesis Testing

My Claim Is about a:	Claim	Assumption	Parametric Test/Statistic	Nonparametric Test/Statistic
mean	Class A has a higher IQ than average.	$n \geq 30$ or s.d. known	Z	Sign Test
		$n < 30$, s.d. unknown	T	Wilcox/Mann-Whitney U (U)
proportion	75% of voters prefer candidate	$np > 5$ and $nq > 5$	Z	
standard deviation	This instrument has fewer errors than others	normal population	x^2	Kruskal-Wallis H (H)
two means	EZ diet is more effective than DF diet? The percent of cures is the same for those using drug A as Drug B.	dependent independent (A low t or U value would indicate that the proportions are similar.)	T T or Z	Sign Test (U)
two standard deviations	The ages of group A are more homogeneous than the ages of group B.		F	(H)
two proportions	There are more Democrats in Chicago than L.A.		Z	Sign Test
relationship between 2 variables	Smoking related to cancer. (If r is close to 0, then no relation)		Pearson r	Spearman r
Are two variables dependent?			F	H
How closely do expected values agree with observed?	k variables (a.k.a. Goodness of Fit)		x^2 df = k – 1	
ANOVA	comparing 3 or more means	(compute: variances between sample means/total variances)	F	Kruskal-Wallis (H)

df: num: = (k – 1) den = k(n – 1); K = no. of groups n = amt in each group

Assumptions for ANOVA: normal distribution, equal variances from each sample. However, George E.P. Box demonstrated that as long as the sample sizes are equal (or near equal) the variances can be up to nine times as large and the results from ANOVA will continue to be essentially reliable. However, if the data don't fit these basic assumptions we can always use the nonparametric version (Kruskal-Wallis). If a significant F ratio is found, another test can be employed to determine where the significance lies. One of these is Tukey's HSD (honestly significant difference).

Contingency table (two–way ANOVA): A table of observed frequencies where the rows correspond to one variable and the columns another. It is used to see if two variables are dependent, but cannot be used to determine what the relationship is between the two variables.

Study of 1000 Deaths of Males

	Cancer	Heart Disease	Other
Smoking	135	310	205
Non-Smoking	55	155	140

Note: The values in the table are observed values. These would be compared to "expected" values. A x^2 statistic would be computed. A large x^2 value indicates there is a relation between variables.

We are now going to examine some felicitous applications for other statistical tests. You might wish to scan the list and see if you can identify similarities between the examples given and any of the hypotheses that you are planning to test.

Cutting Board:

The nonparametric counterpart of both the *t* and *z* tests is the Sign Test or the Mann-Whitney U test.

We are now going to examine some felicitous applications for other statistical tests. You might wish to scan the list and see if you can identify similarities between the examples given and any of the hypotheses that you are planning to test.

Testing Claims about Two Means

In this section we will discuss a claim made about two means (that the mean of one group is less than, greater than, or equal to the mean of another group). The researcher will first need to determine if the groups are dependent, i.e., the values in one sample are related to the values in another sample. This includes before and after tests; tests involving spouses, relationships between an employer and an employee; or if the groups are independent, i.e., the values in one sample are not related to the values in another sample. This includes comparing an experimental group to a control group, or samples from two different populations, such as the eating habits of people in Michigan vs. Hawaii.

If the researcher can answer yes to one of the questions below, then the identical statistical test described in this section can be employed. Is the researcher claiming that:

____1.   One product, program, or treatment is better than another?
____2.   One group is better (or worse) than another? (With respect to some variable.)
____3.   An experimental program was effective?

Many real and practical situations involve testing hypotheses made about two population means. For example, a manufacturer may want to compare output on two different machines to see if they obtain the same result. A nutritionist might wish to compare the weight loss that results from patients on two different diet plans to determine which one is more effective. A psychologist may want to test for a difference in mean reaction times between men and women to determine if women respond more quickly than men in an emergency situation.

If the two samples (groups) are dependent—the values in one sample are related to the values in the other in some way—a t statistic is computed and a simple paired t-test may be used to test your claim. Computing the differences between the related means and then obtaining the mean of all these differences obtain this t-statistic.

If the two samples are independent, i.e., the values in one sample are not related to the values in the other, and the size of each group, n, is 30 or more, or the standard deviations of the population, then a simple z statistic may be computed and a paired z-test could be ordered. In this case, the differences in the population means are computed and subtracted from the differences in the sample means. The result is divided by the square root of the sum of each variance divided by the respective sample size.

BUT if the two samples are independent, the sample size (n) is less than 30 for each group, and the population standard deviation is not known, then whom do you call? The F (team) test. The F test is used first to see if the standard deviations are equal. (A relatively small f value indicates that the standard deviations are the same.) If the f-value is relatively small, then the researcher, or much more likely a computer, would need to perform a t-test to test the claim. This involves a very hackneyed computation. However, if the F-test was to yield a relatively large F value, this would lead to a more benign t-test.

Once the mean and standard deviation are computed for each sample, it is customary to identify the group with the larger standard deviation as group 1 and the other sample as group 2.

The nonparametric counterpart of the paired z or t-test is the Wilcoxan signed-ranks test, if samples are dependent, and the Wilcoxan Rank-Sum Test, if samples are independent.

Testing Claims about Three or More Means

If you can answer yes to one of the questions below, you can use the identical statistical test described in this section. Are you claiming that:

____1.   There is a difference between three or more products, programs, or treatments?
____2.   There are different outcomes from the same program, product, or treatment among three or more different groups?

Claims about three or more means require the creation of an F-statistic and the performing of an F test. Here you, or hopefully your computer, will compare the variances between the samples to the variances within the samples. The nickname for what's happening here is ANOVA (Analysis of Variance). It is an extension of the t-test, which is used for testing two means. The null hypothesis is that the means are equal.

An F value close to 1 would indicate that there are no significant differences between the sample means. A relatively large F value will cause you to reject the null hypothesis and conclude that the means in the samples are not equal. Some important things to know about the F distribution:

1. It is not symmetric, it is skewed to the right.
2. The values of F can be 0 or positive, but not negative.
3. There is a different F distribution for each pair of degrees of freedom for the numerator and denominator.

Note: If you are asking yourself or *The Dissertation and Research Cookbook*, "Why are we dealing with variances when the claim is about means?" you would be asking a very good question. The answer is that the variance, or the standard deviation squared, is determined by, and dependent on, the mean, so it is actually all in the family!

For Your Information and Education

The method of ANOVA owes its beginning to Sir Ronald A. Fisher (1890–1962) and received its early impetus because of its applications to problems in agricultural research. It is such a powerful statistical tool that it has since found applications in just about every branch of scientific research, including economics, psychology, marketing research, and industrial engineering, to mention just a few.

The following example will be testing a claim about three means obtained from a sample using the ssss CANDOALL model. A report on the findings follows the example.

Example: A study was done to investigate the time in minutes for three police precincts to arrive at the scene of a crime. Sample results from similar types of crime are:

A: 7   4   4   3
    sample size: $n = 4$, mean, $x = 4.5$, variance, $s^2 = 3.0$
B: 9   5   7
    sample size: $n = 3$, mean $x = 7.0$, variance, $s^2 = 4.2$
C: 2   3   5   3   8
    sample size: $n = 5$, mean $x = 4.2$, variance, $s^2 = 5.7$

At the $\alpha = 0.05$ significance level, test the claim that the precincts have the same mean reaction time to similar crimes.

What are the pre-test s's and assumptions?

Assumptions for ANOVA: normal distribution, equal variances from each sample. However, George E.P. Box demonstrated that as long as the sample sizes are equal (or near equal) the variances can be up to nine times as large and the results from ANOVA will continue to be essentially reliable.

a. *What is the substantive hypothesis?* (What does the researcher think will happen?)
    The reaction times are similar in the three precincts.

b. *How large is the sample size that was studied?* The three groups have sample sizes 4, 3, and 5 respectively.

c. *What descriptive statistic was determined by the sample?* The means and variances for each group were determined.

Now we are ready to take the information obtained in (a), (b), and (c) and employ the eight step **CANDOALL** recipe to test this hypothesis.

We will determine if the claim "The reaction times are similar" is statistically correct.

1. Identify the **Claim** (C) to be tested and express it in symbolic form.

$$\mu_a = \mu_b = \mu_c$$

That is, there is a claim that the mean reaction time in each precinct is the same.

2. Express in symbolic form the **Alternative** (A) statement that would be true if the original claim is false.

$$\mu_a \neq \mu_b \neq \mu_c$$

Remember we must cover all possibilities.

3. Identify the **Null** (N) and alternative hypothesis.
Note: The null hypothesis should be the one that contains no change (an equal sign).

H_0: $\mu_a = \mu_b = \mu_c$ (Null hypothesis)
H_1: $\mu_a \neq \mu_b \neq \mu_c$ (Alternative hypothesis)

Remember: A statistical test is designed to reject or fail to reject (accept) the statistical null hypothesis being examined.

4. **Decide** (D) on the level of significance, alpha (α), based on the seriousness of a type I error.
Note: This is the mistake of rejecting the null hypothesis when it is in fact true. Make alpha small if the consequences of rejecting a true alpha are severe. The smaller the alpha value, the less likely you will be to reject the null hypothesis. Alpha values 0.05 and 0.01 are very common.

$$\alpha = 0.05$$

5. **Order** (O) a statistical test and sampling distribution that is relevant to the study. (see Table 1)
Since the claim involves data from three groups and we wish to test the hypothesis that the differences among the sample means are due to chance, we can use the ANOVA test.
Note: The following assumptions apply when using the ANOVA: The population has a normal distribution; the populations have the same variance (or standard deviation, or similar sample sizes); the samples are random and independent of each other.

6. Perform the **Arithmetic** (A) and determine: the test statistic, the critical value, and the critical region.
Note: It would be best for this to be performed on a computer.
To perform an ANOVA test we need to compute:
The number of samples, k

$$k = 3$$

The mean of all the times, X

$$x = 5.0$$

The variance between the samples—this is found by subtracting the mean (5.0) from the variance of each sample, squaring the differences, then multiplying each by the sample size and finally adding up the results for each sample.

The variance within the samples—this is found by multiplying the variance of each sample by one less than the number in the sample, adding the results—this equals 39.8—and then dividing by the total population minus the number of samples, 9.

The variance within the samples = 4.4222

The test statistic is $F = \dfrac{\text{variance between samples}}{\text{variance within samples}}$

$$F = 1.8317$$

The variance between the samples = 8.1

The degrees of freedom in the numerator = k − 1 = 3 − 1 = 2. The degrees of freedom in the denominator = n − k = 12 − 3 = 9.

Note: Degrees of freedom are the number of values that are free to vary after certain restrictions have been imposed on all values. For example, if 10 scores must total 80, then we can freely assign values to the first nine scores, but the tenth score would then be determined so that there would be nine degrees of freedom. In a test using an *F* statistic we need to find the degrees of freedom in both the numerator and the denominator.

The critical value of *F* = 4.2565. (This can be found on a table or from a computer program.)

7. **Look** (L) to reject or fail to reject the null hypothesis.

Note: This is a right-tailed test since the *F* statistic yields only positive values.

Since the test statistic of *F* = 1.8317 does not exceed the critical value of *F* = 4.2565, we fail to reject the null hypothesis that the means are equal.

Note: The shape of an *F* distribution is slightly different for each sample size, *n*. The $\alpha = 0.05$ level employs us to find an *F* value that will separate the curve into two unequal regions: the smaller one with an area of 0.05 (5%), and the larger one with an area of 100% − 5% or 95% (0.95). (Often referred to as a 95% confidence level.)

8. In **Lay** terms (L) write what happened.

There is not sufficient sample evidence to warrant rejection of the claim that the means are equal.

Note: In order for statistics to make sense in research it is important to use a rigorously controlled design in which other factors are forced to be constant. The design of the experiment is critically important, and no statistical calisthenics can salvage a poor design.

Writing about This Study in a Research Paper

If this study were to be published in a research journal, the following script could be used to summarize the statistical findings. This information usually appears in the data analysis section of a document but could also be properly placed in the section where the conclusion of the study is found, or even in the methodology section of the paper. This information would also be very appropriate to place in the abstract of the study.

A study was conducted to investigate the time in minutes for three police precincts to arrive at the scene of a crime. Sample results from similar types of crime were found to be:

A: 7   4   4   3
      sample size: $n = 4$, mean, $x, = 4.5$, variance, $s^2 = 3.0$

B: 9   5   7
      sample size: $n = 3$, mean, $x = 7.0$, variance, $s^2 = 4.2$

C: 2   3   5   3   8
      sample size: $n = 5$, mean, $x = 4.2$ variance, $s^2 = 5.7$

At the $\alpha = 0.05$ significance level, the claim that the precincts had the same mean reaction time to similar crimes was tested. The null hypothesis is the claim that the samples come from populations with the same mean:

H_0: $\mu_a = \mu_b = \mu_c$ (Null hypothesis)
H_1: $\mu_a \neq \mu_b \neq \mu_c$ (Alternative hypothesis)

To determine if there are any statistically significant differences between the means of the three groups, an ANOVA test was performed. The groups were similar in size and the level of measurement was ratio data. An F distribution was employed to compare the two different estimates of the variance common to the different groups (i.e., variation between samples, and variation within the samples). A test statistic of $F = 1.8317$ was obtained. With two degrees of freedom for the numerator and nine degrees of freedom for the denominator, the critical F value of 4.2565 was determined. Since the test F does not exceed the critical F value, the null hypothesis was not rejected. There is not sufficient sample evidence to reject the claim that the mean values were equal.

The nonparametric counterpart of ANOVA is the Kruskal-Wallis Test.

Testing a Claim about Proportions/Percentages

If the answer to one of the questions below is "yes," then the identical statistical test described in this section could be employed. Is the researcher claiming that:

____1.   A certain percent or ratio is higher or lower than what is believed?
____2.   There is a characteristic of a group that is actually prevalent in a higher or lower percent?

Data at the nominal (name only) level of measurement lack any real numerical significance and are essentially qualitative in nature. One way to make a quantitative analysis, when qualitative data are obtained, is to represent that data in the form of a percentage or a ratio. This representation is very useful in a variety of applications, including surveys, polls, and quality control considerations involving the percentage of defective parts.

A Z-test will work fine here provided that the size of the population is large enough. The condition is that:

$$np \geq 5 \text{ and } nq \geq 5$$

where, as always, n = sample size, p = population and $q = 1 - p$

Note: The p in the test of proportions is different than the "p-value" we use to determine significance in hypothesis testing. It is important to be aware that in mathematics often times the same symbol can have more than one interpretation. While doing mathematics keep this in mind and remember to learn the meaning of a symbol in its context.

Example: If a manager believes that less than 48% of her employees support the company's dress code, the claim can be checked based on the response of a random sample of employees.

If 720 employees were sampled and 54.2% actually favored the dress code, then to check the manager's claim, the researcher could perform a test of hypothesis to determine if the actual value of 0.542 is significantly different from the value of 0.48. Here, $n = 720$, $p = .48$, $q = 0.542$. The conditions $np \geq 5$ and $nq \geq 5$ are met since $720(.48) = 345.6$ and $720(.542) = 390.24$. The z-value would be 3.33. This would lead us to reject the null hypothesis and conclude that this is probably a low estimate.

Testing Claims about Standard Deviations and Variability

Many real and practical situations demand decisions or inferences about variances and standard deviations. In manufacturing, quality control engineers want to ensure that a product is on the average acceptable but also want to produce items of consistent quality so there are as few defects as possible. Consistency is measured by variances.

For Your Information and Education

During World War II, 35,000 American engineers and technicians were taught to use statistics to improve the quality of war material through the efforts of Dr. W. Edwards Deming (born in Sioux City, Iowa, on October 14, 1900). Deming's work was brought to the attention of the Union of Japanese Scientists and Engineers (JUSE). JUSE called upon Deming to help its members increase productivity. Deming convinced the Japanese people that quality drives profits up. The rebirth of Japanese industry and its worldwide success is attributed to the ideas and the teachings of Deming. In gratitude, the late Emperor Hirohito awarded Japan's Second Order Medal of the Sacred Treasure to Deming.

If you can answer yes to one of the questions below, you can use the identical statistical test described in this section. Are you claiming that:

____1.   A product, program, or treatment has more or less variability than the standard?
____2.   A product, program, or treatment is more or less consistent than the standard?

To test claims involving variability, the researcher usually turns to a chi-square (X^2) statistic.

For Your Information and Education

Both the t and chi-square (X^2) distributions have a slightly different shape depending on n, the number in the sample. For this reason, the researcher needs to determine the "degrees of freedom" to find out what shape curve will be used to obtain the test statistics.

The "degrees of freedom" refer to the number of observations or scores minus the number of parameters that are being studied. (Informally, it is the number of times you can miss a certain targeted number and still have a chance of obtaining that desired outcome.) When the researcher uses a sample size of (n) to investigate one parameter, e.g., a mean or standard deviation, the degrees of freedom equal $n - 1$. When investigating a relationship between two variables, the degrees of freedom are ($n - 2$). The test statistics used in tests of hypothesis involving variances or standard deviations, is chi-square, X^2.

Example: A supermarket finds that the average check-out waiting time for a customer on Saturday mornings is 8 minutes, with a standard deviation of 6.2 minutes. One Saturday management experimented with a single queue. They sampled 25 customers and found that the average waiting time remained 8 minutes, but the standard deviation went down to 3.8 minutes.

To test the claim that the single line causes lower variation in waiting time, a computed chi-square value would be: $X^2 = 9.016$ and there would be 24 degrees of freedom since $n = 25$. The null hypothesis would be that the new line produced a standard deviation of waiting time greater than or equal to 6.2, and this would yield a one-tail (left) test. The critical value would be 13.48, and we would reject the null hypothesis if the computed value were less than the critical value. Since $9.016 < 13.48$ we would reject the null hypothesis and conclude that this method seems to lower the variation in waiting time.

Testing a Claim about the Relation between Two Variables (Correlation and Regression Analysis)

Many real and practical situations demand decisions or inferences about how data from a certain variable can be used to determine the value of some other related variable.

For example, a Florida study of the number of powerboat registrations and the number of accidental manatee deaths confirmed that there was a significant positive correlation. As a result, Florida created coastal sanctuaries where powerboats are prohibited so that manatees could thrive.

A study in Sweden found that there was a higher incidence of leukemia among children who lived within 300 meters of a high-tension power line during a 25-year period. This led Sweden's government to consider regulations that would reduce housing in close proximity to high-tension power lines.

If you can answer yes to the questions below, the researcher can use the identical statistical test described in this section. Is the researcher claiming that:

____1.   There is a relationship or correlation between two factors, two events, or two characteristics **and**

____2.   The data are at least of the interval measure.

In regression and correlation analysis:

1. Data are recorded in table form.
2. A scatter diagram is usually created to see any obvious relationships or trends.
3. The correlation coefficient r (rho), a.k.a. the Pearson Correlation Coefficient factor, is used to obtain objective analysis that will uncover the magnitude and significance of the relationship between the variables.
4. A test is performed to determine if r is statistically significant.
5. If r is statistically significant, regression analysis can be used to determine the relationship between the variables.

Example: Suppose a randomly selected group of teachers is given a test on how they integrate calculators into their classrooms and then tested for their levels of math anxiety using a MARS test.

1. Record information in table form (some of these values appear below):

MARS	SOCU
123.00	15.00
145.00	12.00
154.00	11.00
121.00	16.00
230.00	5.00
300.00	4.00
145.00	10.00
124.00	17.00
145.00	11.00
165.00	12.00
138.00	14.00
312.00	4.00

The researcher's hypothesis is that teachers who have lower levels of math anxiety are more likely to use calculators in their classes. (*Note:* The independent variable, m, is Math Anxiety level, which is being used to predict the dependent variable, s, is the SOCU value which indicates the predicted level of calculator use.)

H_0: $r = 0$ (there is no relationship)
H_1: $r \neq 0$ (there is a relationship)

Note: These will usually be the hypotheses in regression analysis.
2. Draw a scatter diagram:

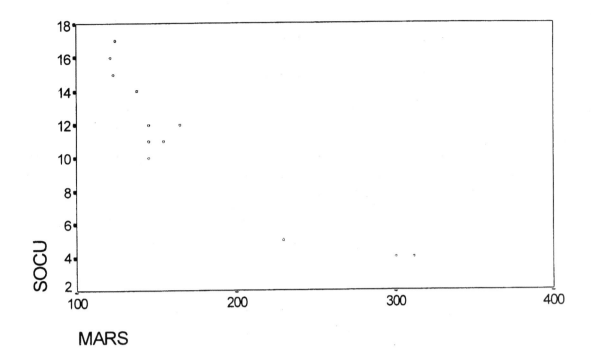

SOCU

MARS

The points in the figure above seem to follow a downward pattern, so we might conclude that there is a relationship between level of math anxiety and the use of calculators by teachers, but this is somewhat subjective.

3. Compute r.

To obtain a more precise and objective analysis we can compute the linear coefficient constant, r. Computing r is a tedious exercise in arithmetic but practically any statistical computer program or scientific calculator would willingly help you along. In our example, the very friendly program SPSS was used to determine that $r = -.882$

Some of the properties of this number r are:

1. The computed value of r must be between (-1) and $(+1)$. (If it's not, then someone or something messed up.)

2. A strong positive correlation would yield an r value close to $(+1)$, a strong negative linear correlation would be close to (-1).

3. If r is close to 0 we conclude that there is no significant linear correlation between x and y.

Checking the table, we find that with a sample size of 10, $(n = 10)$, the value $r = -.9169$ indicating a strong negative correlation between the use of calculators and measures of math anxiety levels. The r-squared number (.779) indicates that a person's math anxiety might explain 84% of their calculator usage (or non-usage).

4. If there is a significant relation, then regression analysis is used to determine what that relationship is. If the relation is linear, the equation of the line of best fit can be determined. (For two variables, the equation of a line can be expressed as y = mx + b, where m is the slope and b is the y intercept.)

Thus, the equation of the line of best fit would be

$$S = -.9169m + 21.614$$

The nonparametric counterpart to r is the Spearman's rank correlation coefficient (r_s) or r.

Cutting Board:

How alike are two people's tastes in television shows? The following activity will employ the nonparametric Spearman rank correlation coefficient test to help determine the answer to this question. You will need a friend or a relative to do this activity.

1. In column I of the chart provided in step 3, list 10 different TV shows that you and a friend or relative are familiar with. Try to have at least one news show, a situation comedy, a mystery, a variety show, a talk show and a drama. Include shows that you like as well as those that you dislike.
2. In column II, rank the shows that are listed, where 1 is your favorite (the one you would be most inclined to watch) and 10 is your least favorite (the one you would be least inclined to watch).
3. Have your friend or relative do a similar ranking in column III.

I TV Shows	II Your Ratings	III F/R Ratings	IV d	V d^2
A.				
B.				
C.				
D.				
E.				
F				
G.				
H.				
I.				
J.				

4. Use the graph that follows to plot the ordered pairs consisting of the two rankings. Label the points with the letters corresponding to the shows in the list. If the two rankings were identical, the points would be on a starting line pointing northeast and forming a 45-degree angle with both axes. If you were in total disagreement then the points would be on a straight line pointing southeast and also form a 45-degree angle with both axes.

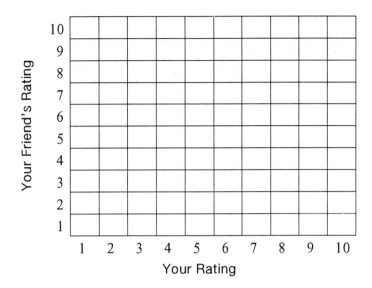

5. Although the scattergram you created might give you an impression of how the two ratings match or correlate with each other, it is probably not very definitive. To determine how closely correlated these rankings are, we can use the r statistics and the Spearman rank correlation coefficient, which we will compute in the steps that follow.

6. Go back to the chart in step 2 and compute d, the difference between the two ratings for each show, and d^2 that is (d)(d). After you have all the d^2s, add them up.

7. The formula for finding the rank correlation is:

$$r_s = 1 - \frac{6 \sum d^2}{n(n^2 - 1)}$$

8. To do this on your calculator, multiply the sum of your d^2 numbers by 6. Divide this product by 990, which is the denominator, (10)(99). Store this number in memory +. Compute 1 minus memory recall. The number in the display is your r number. It should be between −1 and +1.

9. A Spearman table indicates that for your sample size of 10, an r-value of .564 or greater would indicate a positive correlation with an alpha of 0.10, or a negative value less than −.564 would indicate a negative correlation with an alpha value of 0.10. The closer r is to 1 or −1, the stronger the relation. An r-value close to 0 indicates no particular relation. What can you conclude from this test? Should you and this other person turn on the tube when you are together or would it be better to find a different activity?

Critical Values of Spearman's Rank Correlation Coefficient, r_s

n	$\alpha = 0.10$	$\alpha = 0.05$	$\alpha = 0.02$	$\alpha = 0.01$
10	.564	.648	.745	.794

For more on creating scatterplots see: http://www.stat.berkeley.edu/~stark/Java/correlation.htm.

More on Correlational Analysis [Warning: Correlation does not imply CAUSATION!]

The purpose of correlational research is to find co-relationships between two or more variables with the hope of better understanding the conditions and events we encounter and of making predictions about the future. (From the Annals of Chaos Theory: Predictions are usually very difficult—especially if they are about the future; predictions are like diapers, both need to be changed often and for the same reason!)

As was noted previously, the linear correlation coefficient, r, measures the strength of the linear relationship between two paired variables in a sample. If there is a linear correlation, that is, if r is large enough, between two variables, then regression analysis is used to identify the relationship with the hope of predicting one variable from the other.

Note: If there is no significant linear correlation, then a regression equation cannot be used to make predictions.

A regression equation based on old data is not necessarily valid now. The regression equation relating used car prices and ages of cars is no longer usable if it is based on data from the 1960s. Often a scattergram is plotted to get a visual view of the correlation and possible regression equation.

Note: Nonlinear relationships can also be determined, but due to the fact that more complex mathematics are used to describe and interpret data, they are used considerably less often. The following are characteristics of all linear correlational studies:

1. Main research questions are stated as null hypotheses, i.e., no relationship exists between the variables being studied.
2. In simple correlation, there are two measures for each individual in the sample.
3. To apply parametric methods, there must be at least 30 individuals in the study.
4. They can be used to measure the degree of relationships, not simply whether a relationship exists.
5. A perfect positive correlation is 1.00; a perfect negative (inverse) is –1.00.
6. A correlation of 0 indicates no linear relationship exists.
7. If, when two variables x and y are correlated so that $r = .5$, then we say that $(0.5)^2$ or 0.25 or 25% of their variation is common, or variable x can predict 25% of the variance in y.

Bivariate correlation is when there are only two variables being investigated. The following definitions help us determine which statistical test can be used to determine correlation and regression.

Continuous scores: Scores can be measured using a rational scale.
Ranked data: Likert Scale, class rankings.
Dichotomy: Subjects classified into two categories—Republican vs. Democrat.
Artificial: Pass/fail (arbitrary decision), true dichotomy (male/female).

The Pearson Product Moment Correlation Coefficient (that is a mouthful!) or simply the Pearson r, is the most common measure of the strength of the linear relationship between two variables. It is named for Karl Pearson (1857–1936) who originally developed it. The Spearman Rank Correlation Coefficient, or Spearman r, (which we performed above), used for ranked data or when you have a sample size less than 30 ($n < 30$), is the second most popular measure the strength of the linear relationship between two variables. To measure of the strength of the linear relationship between test items for reliability purposes, the Cronbach alpha is the most efficient method of measuring the internal consistency. The following is a table to determine what statistical technique is best used with respect to the type of data the researcher collects.

Technique	Symbol	Variable 1	Variable 2	Remarks
Pearson	r	Continuous	Continuous	Smallest standard of error
Spearman Rank	r	Ranks	Ranks	Used also when n < 30
Kendall's tau	t	Ranks	Ranks	Used for n < 10
Biserial Correlation (Cronbach)	a/bis	Artificial Dichotomy	Continuous	Sometimes exceeds 1, often used in item analysis.
Widespread biserial correlation	r/wbis	Artificial Dichotomy	Continuous Interval	Looking for extremes on Variable 1
Point-biserial correlation	r/pbis	True dichotomy	Continuous Interval	Yields lower correlation than r/biserial
Tetrachoric correlation	r/t	Artificial Dichotomy	Artificial Dichotomy	Used when Var 1 and 2 can be split arbitrarily (example: self-confidence vs. Internal Locus of Control)
Phi coefficient	$\varnothing$	True Dichotomy	Artificial Dichotomy	
Correlation ratio eta	h	Continuous	Continuous	Nonlinear Relationships

Multivariate Correlational Statistics

If you wish to test a claim that multiple independent variables might be used to make a prediction about a dependent variable, you have several possible tests that can be constructed. Such studies involve **Multivariate Correlational Statistics.**

Discriminate analysis: Used to determine the correlation between two or more predictor variables and a dichotomous criterion variable. The main use of discriminant analysis is to predict group membership (e.g., success/non-success) from a set of predictors. If a set of variables is found which provide satisfactory discrimination, classification equations can be derived, their use checked out through hit/rate tables, and if good, they can be used to classify new subjects who were not in the original analysis. In order to use discriminate analysis certain assumptions (conditions) must be met:

- At least twice the number of subjects as variables in study.
- Each groups has at least n = # of variables.
- Groups have the same variance/covariance structures.
- All variables are normally distributed.

Canonical correlation: Used to predict a combination of several criterion variables from a combination of several predictor variables.

Path analysis: Used to test theories about hypothesized causal links between variables that are correlated.

Factor analysis: Used to reduce a large number of variables to a few factors by combining variables that are moderately or highly correlated with one another.

Differential analysis: Used to examine correlation between variables among homogeneous subgroups within a sample, can be used to identify moderator variables that improve a measure's predictive validity.

Multiple regression: Used to determine the correlation between a criterion variable and a combination of two or more predictor variables. As in any regression method we need the following conditions to be met: We are investigating linear relationships; for each x value, y is a random variable having a normal distribution. All of the y variables have the same variance; for a given value of x, the distribution of y values has a mean that lies on the regression line.

Note: Results are not seriously affected if departures from normal distributions and equal variances are not too extreme.

The following example illustrates how a researcher might use different multivariate correlational statistics in a research project.

Example: Suppose a researcher has, among other data, scores on three measures for a group of teachers working overseas:

1. Years of experience as a teacher.
2. Extent of travel while growing up.
3. Tolerance for ambiguity.

Research question: Can these measures (or other factors) predict the degree of adaptation to the overseas culture they are working on?

Discriminate analysis: Hypothesis (1) The outcome is dichotomous between those who adapted well and those who adapted poorly based on these three measures. Hypothesis (2) Knowing these three factors could be used to predict success.

Multiple regression: Hypothesis: Some combination of the three predictor measures correlates better with predicting the outcome measure than any one predictor alone.

Canonical correlation: Hypothesis: Several measures of adaptation could be quantified, i.e., adaptation to food, climate, customs, etc., based on these predictors.

Path analysis. Hypothesis: Childhood travel experience leads to tolerance for ambiguity and desire for travel as an adult, and this makes it more likely that teachers will score high on these predictors, which will lead them to seek an overseas teaching experience and adapt well to the experience.

Factor analysis: Suppose there are five more (a total of eight) adaptive measures that could be determined. All eight measures can be examined to determine whether they cluster into groups such as education, experience, personality traits, etc.

Example: To compute the correlation between gender (male/female) and employment status (employed/unemployed) you could use a phi coefficient. You couldn't use it for age and income, however, because these are not dichotomous variables.

Example: A Kendall's tau could be used to compute the correlation between feelings about a new health plan (not in favor/in favor/highly in favor) and health of a patient (unhealthy/healthy/very healthy).

Example: A Point Biserial correlation can be used when females and males applying for a job report the total number of years of education they have had, and we want to know whether there is any correlation between gender and years of education.

Analysis of Covariance

A "yes" on question one below will lead you to a different type of statistical test involving bivariate data. Are you claiming that:

____1.   Two groups being compared come from the same population and contain similar characteristics?

If you are planning to divide your subjects into two groups (perhaps a control group and an experimental group), or if you are planning to use two different treatments on two different groups, then problems in randomization and matching the groups might be a concern.

A relatively new statistical process called analysis of covariance (ANCOVA) has been developed to equate the groups on certain relevant variables identified prior to the investigation. Pre-test mean scores are often used as covariates.

The following guidelines should be used in the analysis of covariance:

1.   The correlation of the covariate (some variable different than the one you are testing) and the response variable should be statistically and educationally significant.
2.   The covariate should have a high reliability.
3.   The covariate should be a variable that is measured prior to any portions of the treatments.
4.   The conditions of homogeneity of regression should be met. The slopes of the regression lines describing the linear relationships of the criterion variable and the covariate from cell to cell must not be statistically different.
5.   All follow-up procedures for significant interaction or post-hoc comparisons should be made with the adjusted cell or adjusted marginal means.

ANCOVA is a transformation from raw scores to adjusted scores, which take into account the effects of the covariate. ANCOVA allows us to compensate somewhat when groups are selected by non-random methods.

The nonparametric counterpart of ANCOVA is the Runs Test.

If your hypothesis is that many variables or factors are contributing to a certain condition, you may wish to use multiple regression analysis. This is similar to linear regression analysis with a significant increase in number crunching. If this is not how you wish to spend several hours of your day, we recommend that you employ a computer to crank out the numerical information necessary to use multiple regression analysis.

Contingency Tables

If you only want to test:

____1.   Whether two variables are dependent on one another (e.g., are death and smoking dependent variables; are SAT scores and high school grades independent variables?).

You might consider using a contingency table.

The null hypothesis would be that the variables are independent. Setting up a contingency table is easy; the rows are one variable, the columns another. In contingency table analysis you determine how closely the amount in each cell coincides with the expected value of each cell if the two variables were independent.

The following contingency table lists the response to a bill pertaining to gun control.

	In Favor	Opposed
Northeast	10	30
Southeast	15	25
Northwest	35	10
Southwest	10	25

Notice that cell 1 indicates that 10 people in the Northeast were in favor of the bill.

Example: In the previous contingency table, 40 out of 160 (1/4) of those surveyed were from the Northeast. If the two variables were independent, you would expect 1/2 of that number (20) to be in favor of the amendment since there were only two choices.

To determine how close the expected values are to the actual values, the test statistic chi-square is determined. Small values of chi-square support the claim of independence between the two variables. That is, chi-square will be small when observed and expected frequencies are close. Large values of chi-square would cause the null hypothesis to be rejected and reflect significant differences between observed and expected frequencies.

Before you move into your final phase, use the cutting board below to assist you in deciding what spices you can use in your study.

Cutting Board:

1. Underline the terms that best complete the sentence. I will be testing a claim about a mean, a standard deviation, a proportion, 2 means, 2 variances, a relationship between 2 variables, the independence of 2 variables, relationship between more than 2 variables.
2. If you will be using nonparametric testing, underline the test(s) that you think you will use (you might wish to read the information on nonparametrics first). Sign Test, Wilcoxon Signed-Ranks, Wilcoxon Rank-Sum Test, Kruskal-Wallis Test, Spearman Rank Correlation, Runs Test, Friedman, McNemear, Mann-Whitney U, Fisher.
3. If you plan to use parametric testing, underline the test(s) that you plan to use. Z test, t-test, paired t or z test, x^2, r, F-test, Pearson, other: _____
4. Why did you choose the test(s) in 2 and/or 3?
   After your data are collected, make sure you sojourn through this section again and fill out all information relevant to your research study. Once this is accomplished, you will be able to "fully digest" Chapter 4 of your dissertation.

TEST YOUR QUANTITATIVE ACUMEN

1. Descriptive Statistics

A) The consistency with which the same results occur.

2. Ex Post Facto

B) Experimental studies that are not "double-blind" and might cause bias on the part of the researcher.

3. Inferential Statistics	C) A mode of inquiry in which a theory is proposed and hypotheses are made in advance of gathering data about a specific phenomenon. Hypothetical-deductive theory.
4. Factorial Design	D) A form of descriptive research in which the investigator looks for relationships that may explain phenomena that have already taken place.
5. A Priori	E) A method used to depict systematically the facts and characteristics of a given population or area of interest.
6. Validity	F) Differences in independent variables relevant to a study are controlled.
7. Reliability	G) A method that rigorously explores the efficacy of a program, treatment, or product.
8. Rosenthal Effect	H) A method used to study the effects of more than one independent variable on more than one dependent variable.
9. Hawthorne Effect	I) A set of procedures used to test hypotheses or estimate the parameters in a population.
10. Quasi-Experimental	J) Subjects appear to make progress just because they are subjects.
11. Covariant Analysis	K) A method in which a sample of convenience is used and then treated to determine if there are any significant differences pre- and post-treatment.
12. Evaluative Research	L) The extent to which data measure what they purport to.

Ans. 1-E, 2-D, 3-I, 4-H, 5-C, 6-L, 7-A, 8-B, 9-J, 10-K, 11-F, 12-G

Nonparametric Tests

To understand the idea of *nonparametric* statistics (the term *nonparametric* was first used by Wolfowitz, 1952) first requires a basic understanding of parametric statistics that we have just studied in some detail. The concept of statistical significance testing is based on the sampling distribution of a particular statistic as well as a basic knowledge of the underlying distribution of a variable. Then we can make predictions about how, in repeated samples of equal size, this particular statistic will "behave," that is, how it is distributed. For example, if we draw 100 random samples of 100 female children of age ten each from the general population, and compute the mean height in each sample, then the distribution of the standardized means across samples will likely approximate the normal distribution. Now imagine that we take an additional sample in a particular city ("Kidysville") where we suspect that 10-year-old girls are taller than the average population. If the mean height in that sample falls outside the upper 95% tail area of the z distribution then we conclude that, indeed, the 10-year-old children of Kidysville are taller than the average population.

In the above example we relied on our knowledge that, in repeated samples of equal size, the standardized means (for height) will be distributed following the z distribution (with a particular mean and variance). However, this will only be true if in the population the variable of interest (height in our example) is normally distributed, that is, if the distribution of people of particular heights follows the normal distribution (the bell-shape distribution).

For many variables of interest, we simply do not know for sure that this is the case. For example, is income distributed normally in the population? Probably not. The incidence of AIDS is not normally distributed in the population, the number of car accidents is not, and neither are many other variables in which a researcher might be interested. Another factor that often limits the applicability of tests based on the assumption that the sampling distribution is normal is the size of the sample of data available for the analysis (*sample size*, *n*). We can assume that the sampling distribution is normal even if we are not sure that the distribution of the variable in the population is normal, as long as our sample is large enough (e.g., 100 or more observations). However, if our sample is very small, then those tests can be used only if we are sure that the variable is normally distributed, and there is often no way to test this.

Hopefully, after this somewhat lengthy overture, the need is evident for statistical procedures that allow us to process data of low quality from small samples, on variables about which nothing is known (concerning their distribution). Specifically, nonparametric methods were developed to be used in cases when the researcher knows nothing about the parameters of the variable of interest in the population (hence the term *nonparametric*). In more technical terms, nonparametric methods do not rely on the estimation of parameters (such as the mean or the standard deviation) describing the distribution of the variable of interest in the population. Therefore, these methods are also sometimes (and more appropriately) called *parameter-free* or *distribution-free* methods.

Advantages of Nonparametric Methods

1. They can be applied to a wide variety of situations since they do not require normally distributed populations.
2. They can be applied to nominal data.
3. Computations are usually simpler.
4. They tend to be easier to understand.

Disadvantages of Nonparametric Methods

1. They tend to waste data. Exact numerical data are reduced to qualitative form.
2. They are less sensitive, therefore we need stronger evidence to reject null hypotheses.

A few of the most popular parametric tests, their nonparametric equivalents, and the efficacy of the nonparametric tests are found in the table that follows.

Application	Parametric Test	Nonparametric Test	Efficacy of Nonparametric Test with Normal Population
Two dependent samples	*t*-test or *z*-test	Sign Test or Wilcoxon signed rank-sum	0.63
Two independent samples	*t*-test or *z*-test	Wilcoxon rank-sum	0.95
Several independent samples	ANOVA (F-test)	Kruskal-Wallis test	0.95
Correlation	Linear - Pearson	Rank Correlation - Spearman	0.95
One sample against a population	*t*-test or *z*-test	Mann-Whitney U	
Change in Nominal Data		McNemar Test	

The Sign Test is one of the easiest nonparametric tests to use. It is based on plus and minus signs, which are easily found. It can be used to test claims involving: The Sign Test is the oldest of all nonparametric statistical tests. It is commonly used in a before-and-after experiment where the researcher can simply assign "a +" to each case where the results were higher after treatment and "a" when the opposite were true.

To use the Sign Test we need two dependent samples. It can be used with any type of data where a change can be determined.

Example: Fourteen right-handed pilots were tested to determine if there was a difference between reaction times using their right and left hand. Use a 0.05 significance level to test the claim of no difference in reaction times.

Right:	189	97	116	165	116	129	171	155	112	102	188	158	121	133
Left:	220	171	121	191	130	134	168	187	123	111	180	186	143	156
Sign of diff:	−	−	−	−	−	−	+	−	−	−	+	−	−	−

Using the s^3d^2, CANDOALL: Decide on test: Sign Test. Arithmetic. Determine x, the number of times the less frequent sign occurs. Twelve negative and two positive give us $x = 2$. This is a two-tailed test since we are testing to see if there is a difference between using the right or left hand. The table below comes from a Critical Sign Test chart. We will reject the null hypothesis (fail to accept the null hypothesis) if x is less than or equal to the value in the table. Since $2 < 3$ we reject the null and conclude that there is reason to believe there is a difference in reaction time.

Critical Values for the Sign Test

n	.005 (one tail) or .01 (two tails)	.01 (one tail) or .02 (two tails)	.025 (one tail) or .05 (two tails)	.05 (one tail) or .10 (two tails)
14	1	2	2	3

Example: A sign test can be used to compare participants' attitudes about purchasing a software program (interested or not interested), before and after having viewed a demonstration of the software.

The Wilcoxon Rank Sum Test

The Wilcoxon rank sum test can be considered a nonparametric equivalent of the unpaired t-test. It is used to test the hypothesis that two independent samples have come from the same population. Because it is nonparametric, it makes no assumptions about the distribution of the data.

An example of the sort of data for which this test could be used is responses on a Likert scale (e.g., 1 = totally disagree, 2 = disagree, 3 = no opinion, 4 = agree, 5 = totally agree). It would be inappropriate to use the t-test for such data because they are only of an ordinal nature. The t-test would test the hypothesis that the means of the two groups differ, but the mean is not a sensible statistic to use for data of this kind. The Wilcoxon rank sum test tells us more generally whether one group is "better" than the other.

The way the test works is to rank all the data from both groups. Thus, the smallest value will be given a rank of 1, the second smallest will have a rank of 2, and so on. Where values are tied, they are given an average rank. The ranks for each group are added together (hence the term *rank sum test*). The sums of the ranks used to be compared with tabulated critical values to generate a p value in the old days, although now a computer would generally do the test. However, for small sample sizes it is still perfectly feasible to do the test manually if you don't have the necessary software.

For example, suppose we are interested in whether a particular drug given for depression affects the liver enzyme ALT. If we measure the study subjects' ALT before and after they take the drug, we have matching pairs of data. We might think of testing the data with a paired *t*-test, but this would not be appropriate because ALT values are not normally distributed. The Wilcoxon signed rank test can be used instead.

The test works as follows: For each subject, we subtract the post-drug ALT value from the pre-drug value. This gives us a number for each subject which may be positive, negative, or zero. We then rank all those numbers in order, ignoring the sign. Finally, we add the ranks of the positive numbers and the ranks of the negative numbers. The summed ranks can then, if need be, be compared with tabulated critical values to generate a *p*-value, although it would be far more likely that the test would be done by appropriate software like your SPSS program.

Example: Comparison of student attitudes about school (very excited, moderately excited, neutral, moderately bored, very bored) before and after taking a course on study habits.

Examples of Other Nonparametric Statistical Tests

The McNemar Test

- Basically, the philosophy of the McNemar Test is similar to that of the chi-square test. It assumes that you are dealing with research questions where two variables are related. Here, our hypothesis usually is that the difference is significant between the pre-condition and post-condition in the same groups.
- The McNemar Test can be used with either nominal or ordinal data and is especially useful with before/after measurement of the same subjects.
- The McNemar Test determines the significance of any observed change by setting up a fourfold table of frequencies to represent the first and second responses.

Example: Suppose a group was interested in the support for a new mental health clinic in a certain area. A town meeting was held to discuss the pros and cons of such a clinic in the area. Participants were surveyed before and after the town meeting.

In the table that follows, A represents those who were in favor before and not in favor after, B represents those who were in favor before *and* after, C not in favor before and not in favor after, and D not in favor before and in favor after. A + D represents the number who changed their minds. Since the data are nominal and the study involves before/after measurements of two related samples, the McNemar test can be used to see if the change from one point of view is different from the change to the other point of view (i.e., is there is a difference between A and D). The null hypothesis would be there is no change. If the test value is higher than the critical value we would reject the null hypothesis.

Before/After	Do not Favor	Favor
Favor	A	B
Oppose	C	D

The chi-square distribution is used for this test. The test value is:

$$X^2 = \frac{(|A - D| - 1)^2}{A + D} \text{ with d.f.} = 1$$

Compute the test chi-square $= [(|A - D| - 1]^2/(A + D)$ and compare the value obtained to the critical value of 3.84. If the test value > 3.84, reject the null; otherwise fail to reject the null.

Example: High school students are surveyed on their knowledge of family planning and birth control. Half the group is given a workshop on this topic. The survey is re-administered to both groups after the seminar to assess the knowledge gained.

Kruskal-Wallis Test

We used analysis of variance (ANOVA) to test hypotheses that influences among several (k) sample means are due to chance. That parametric F test requires that all the involved populations possess normal distributions with variances that are approximately equal. The Kruskal-Wallis test is a nonparametric alternative that does not require normal distributions. In using the Kruskal-Wallis test (also called the H test) we test the null hypothesis that independent and random samples come from the same or identical populations. We compute the test statistic, H, which has a distribution that can be approximated by the chi-square distribution with k – 1 degrees of freedom, as long as each sample has at least five observations.

To use the Kruskal-Wallis Test you must have at least three samples, all of which are random; test the null hypothesis that the samples come from; have identical populations; have each sample contain at least five observations.

The computation of an H value involves considering all observations as if they came from the same group and ranking the entire group from lowest to highest and, in cases of ties, assign to each observation the mean of the ranks involved. Then return each number to its sample and find the sum of the ranks and the sample size.

Example: The income from a random sample of 10 parents at five different schools in one school district is collected to test the claim that the income level of the schools are different.

Fisher's Exact-test

In the Fisher's Exact-test we compute a test statistic for measures of association that relate two **nominal** variables. It is used mainly in 2x2 frequency tables when the expected frequency is too small to trust the use of the chi-square test. A phi (φ) coefficient can be generated which is a symmetric measure equivalent to a Pearson's correlation coefficient.

One of the limitations of the Fisher's Exact-test is that the data must be dichotomous and the elements must originate from two different sources. To compute the correlation between sex (male/female) and employment status (employed/unemployed), you could use a phi coefficient. However, this cannot be used with age and income, since these are not dichotomous variables.

A 2 x 2 contingency table is constructed and usually set up as follows:

	Accepted into SW Program	Rejected from SW Program	Total
From the East	9	2	11
From the West	7	6	13
Total	16	8	24

TABLE $= [9, 2, 7, 6]$
Left: p-value $= 0.9725849149728539$
Right: p-value $= 0.15574101494144757$
2-Tail: p-value $= 0.21079553102705903$

Conclusion: There would be no reason to believe that, based on the data, a person from the West was more likely to be accepted into an SW program. Computations are based on factorials, which become prohibitive if the numbers get large. 8! = 40,320!!!

Example: Compare attitudes toward marijuana (harmful or not harmful) of twelfth graders who did (n = 9) and did not (n = 6) complete a DARE program in elementary school.

Chi-Square Test of Independence

The most familiar use of the chi-square test is when a researcher wants to see if there are statistical differences between the observed (actual) frequencies, and the expected (hypothesized) frequencies of two variables presented in a cross-tabulation or contingency table. The larger the observed frequency is in comparison with the expected frequency, the larger the chi-square statistic is and the more likely the difference is statistically significant.

For example, suppose a researcher gave a pass/fail test of knowledge of drug abuse to a sample of 100 subjects—42 men and 58 women—and 61 subjects passed and 39 failed. Suppose the researcher was interested in whether the differences in knowledge were related to gender. She could use the chi-square test to test the null hypothesis of not statistically significant differences between sexes.

The following tables could be tabulated:

Expected Frequencies

	Pass	Fail	Total
Men	27	15	42
Women	35	23	58
Total	61	39	100

Observed Frequencies

	Pass	Fail	Total
Men	18	24	42
Women	42	16	58
Total	61	39	100

Comparing these tables we see immediately that they are not identical, but were these differences statistically significant? A chi-square test would tell us that the differences are significant at the 0.01 level of significance, leading us to not accept the null hypothesis and conclude that the differences are greater than what could be expected by chance alone.

Assumptions in Using Chi-Square Test of Goodness of Fit

- The sample values are independent and identically distributed.
- The sample values are grouped in categories, and the counts of the number of sample values occurring in each category are recorded.
- The hypothesized distribution is specified in advance, so that the number of observations that should appear for each category, assuming the hypothesized distribution is the correct one, can be calculated without reference to the sample values.

- Guidance: The chi-square test involves using the chi-square distribution to approximate the underlying exact distribution. The approximation becomes better as the expected cell frequencies grow larger, and may be inappropriate for tables with very small expected cell frequencies. For tables with expected cell frequencies less than 5, the chi-square approximation may not be reliable.

A standard (and conservative) rule to follow is to avoid using the chi-square test for tables with expected cell frequencies less than 1, or when more than 20% of the table cells have expected cell frequencies less than 5.

Koehler and Larntz (1980) suggested that if the total number of observations is at least 10, the number of categories is at least 3, and the square of the total number of observations is at least 10 times the number of categories, then the chi-square approximation should be reasonable.

A key assumption of the chi-square test of independence is that each subject contributes data to only one cell. Therefore the sum of all cell frequencies in the table must be the same as the number of subjects in the experiment. Consider an experiment in which each of 12 subjects threw a dart at a target once using his or her preferred hand and once using his or her non-preferred hand. The data are shown below:

	Hit	Missed
Preferred Hand	9	3
Non-preferred Hand	4	8

It would not be valid to use the chi-square test of independence on these data since each subject contributed data to two cells: one cell based on their performance with their preferred hand and one cell based on their performance with their non-preferred hand. The total of the cell frequencies in the table is 24 but the total number of subjects is only 12.

In the test for independence, the claim is that the row and column variables are independent of each other. This is the null hypothesis. The multiplication rule states that if two events were independent, then the probability of both occurring is the product of their probabilities. This is the theory upon which the test of independence is based. If we reject the null hypothesis then it is assumed that the assumption is wrong and the row and column variable are dependent. There is an excellent application of this test at *http://www.psychstat.smsu.edu/introbook/sbk28m.htm*

Mann-Whitney U

This is a nonparametric test to determine if there is a difference between two groups. It is used when the data for two samples are measured on an ordinal scale in rank order. It is the nonparametric equivalent of the *t*-test. Although ordinal measures are used, it is assumed that data are continuously distributed.

The most common test in research is probably a *t*-test for uncorrelated means. However, there are times when the assumptions for this test cannot be met, or times when ordinal (ranked) data are collected and the researcher needs to do a nonparametric test. The *Mann-Whitney U Test* is one of the most popular of the nonparametrics. There is no such thing as a free lunch, of course, so the Mann-Whitney U is less powerful (more conservative, or less likely to find a difference if a real difference exists) than a *t*-test.

It is for:

1. Independently drawn random samples, the sizes of which need not be the same.
2. Samples where the largest is nine or more.

(If both sample sizes are eight or fewer measures, then other tests can be applied.)
Like a Kruskal-Wallis, the Mann-Whitney U works by first ranking the data.

The way it works is that the scores in both groups are combined into one data set ranked from lowest to highest. The rank of each score is recorded and when two or more scores are tied, all of the tied scores get the same rank—a rank equal to the average of the positions in the ordered array. For example, if three scores are tied for position 3, 4, and 5, all would be assigned the rank of 4. If the sums of the ranks are very different, the p-value will be small.

The p-value answers this question: If the populations really have the same median, what is the chance that random sampling would result in a sum of ranks as far apart (or more so) as observed in this experiment?

Example: A group of students were given a sensitivity test and their scores were ranked by gender as follows.

Rank numbers for males: 1, 2, 3, 7, 8, 9, 10, 13, 14, 15, 23, 24, 26, 27
Rank numbers for females: 4, 5, 6, 11, 12, 16, 17, 18, 19, 20, 21, 22, 25, 28, 29, 30, 31

The sum of the rank numbers for males equals 182 (1 + 2 + 3 + 7 + 8 + . . . + 26 + 27), while the sum of the rank number for females equals 314 (4 + 5 + 6 + 11 + . . . + 30 + 31).

The expected sums for males and females are 224 and 272, respectively, the standard deviation of the expected sums is 25.19, and the p-value of the observed divergence equals 0.04779. Thus, at the 0.05 level of significance, we can conclude that females tend toward the higher rank numbers while males tend toward the lower rank numbers.

Example: Determine if the level of physical abuse (minor, moderate, or severe) inflicted by fathers (n = 50) is different from that inflicted by mothers (n = 50) on their court-dependent children.

The Cochran Q Test and the Friedman Test

Recall that the philosophy of the McNemar Test is similar to that of the chi-square test. It assumes that you are dealing with research questions where two variables are related. Here, our hypothesis usually is that the difference *is* significant between the pre-condition and post-condition in the same group's responses. The Cochran Q test is an extension for studies having more than two samples. It tests the hypothesis that the proportion of cases in a category is equal for several related categories. The object of the Cochran test is to investigate the significance of the differences between many treatments (k) on the same n elements with a binomial distribution. Some of the limitations of this test are that it is assumed that there are k series of observations on the same n elements. The observations are dichotomous and 0 or 1 represents the observations in the two classes. In addition, the number of elements must be sufficiently large, usually greater than 10.

The test statistics computed are referred to as a Q-value. This approximately follows a chi-square distribution with k – 1 degrees of freedom. The null hypothesis that the k samples come from one common dichotomous distribution is rejected if Q is larger than the critical value.

When the data are at least ordinal, the Friedman two-way analysis of variance is appropriate. The object of the Friedman test for multiple treatments of a series of subjects is to investigate the significance of the differences in responses for several treatments (k) applied to several subjects (n). It tests matched samples, ranking each case and calculating the mean rank for each variable across all cases. It uses these ranks to compute a test statistic. The product is a two-way table where the rows represent subjects and the columns represent the treatment conditions.

110

Characteristics: The *Friedman test* is frequently called a *two-way analysis on ranks*. It is at the same time a generalization of the Sign-Test and the Spearman Rank Correlation Test. The *Friedman test* models the ratings of *n* (rows) judges on *k* (columns) treatments. One popular application of the Friedman test is found in *wine tastings*, where each judge rates a collection of wines independently of the other judges. The null hypothesis would be that the ratings of the judges are not related (e.g., they cannot distinguish the wines).

The limitation of the Friedman test is that we need to assume that a subject's response to one treatment is not affected by the same subject's response to another treatment; and that the response distribution for each subject is continuous. The test statistic is often referred to as a G value. If this value exceeds the critical chi-square value obtained from a chi-square table with $k - 1$ degrees of freedom, the null hypothesis that the effects of the *k* treatments are all the same is rejected.

If ties occur in the ranking procedure one has to assign the average rank for each series of equal results. For example, 4 entries can be assigned the rank of 12.25.

How the Friedman Test Works The Friedman test is a nonparametric test that compares three or more paired groups. The Friedman test first ranks the values in each matched set (each row) from low to high. Each row is ranked separately. It then sums the ranks in each group (column). If the sums are very different, the *p*-value will be small (and the null hypothesis will be rejected). The whole point of using a matched test is to control for experimental variability between subjects, thus increasing the power of the test. Some factors you don't control in the experiment will increase (or decrease) all the measurements in a subject. Since the Friedman test ranks the values in each row, it is not affected by sources of variability that equally affect all values in a row (since that factor won't change the ranks within the row).

Example: If clinical therapists take part in a new intervention program on drug abuse and their attitudes about this program are measured before the program, during, and after, and they are asked if this program is worthwhile, the Cochran's Q could test the hypothesis that the proportion of "strongly agree" responses will differ for the clinicians taking part in the intervention depending on which of the 3 time periods is being considered. The Friedman test could be used to test the hypothesis. There will be at least one difference among the median attitude scores at pre-intervention, at post-intervention, and at a 6-month follow-up for the clinicians who took part in the intervention.

Example: Children who are living in a residential program return to their families after staying for 3 months, 6 months, or 12 months. The Cochran's Q test can be used to determine if there is a difference in the level of comfort in taking home a family member after these time periods. The Friedman's test could be used to determine if there is a difference in the Family Satisfaction scores of 64 children who were discharged from the residential treatment center at these different time intervals.

The 4 P's: Preliminary Preparation and Proposal Planning (A Recipe for the Construction of a Dissertation Research Proposal)

Before you actually do your research, most graduate programs require that you first put together a research proposal. When done properly, this can provide you with a plan and most of the ingredients you will need to complete a high quality dissertation. Most universities require that you submit a three-chapter proposal, which can later be transformed (with some modification) into the first three chapters of your dissertation.

A dissertation proposal must contain sufficient detail to convince faculty readers that the proposed investigation: 1) has potential to contribute valuable knowledge to the field, 2) is sufficiently planned to assure that the project can be completed (answers research questions) as described in the proposal document, and 3) will possess the level of intellectual rigor commonly expected at the graduate level of study.

In the proposal you will discuss things that you are *going to do* (use the future tense); in the dissertation you write about things you *have done* (past tense). According to Dr. Robert E. Hoye of Walden University, "the most important aspect of writing a proposal is the need to ensure that all of the parts of the proposal fit together. You cannot change your methodology without adjusting the purpose and the significance. The review of literature has to be related to the problem and the hypothesis."

Warning! Any time you change one thing in your proposal (or dissertation) you must make sure than any other part of your design with which it is associated is appropriately modified.

In Phase 3 we will examine how to "cook up" both a terrific proposal (what you will do) and a "delicious" dissertation (what you did do). Many of the suggestions presented here were first seen in Phase 1.

Cutting Board:

Carefully examine the following sample prospectus, and then carefully put together a prospectus for your research proposal. Make sure you share this with the members of your committee and those who will be closely involved with approving your research.

Sample Blue Print (Prospectus) for a Proposal

The application of the 12-step program by alcoholics who have been successful in after care.

Problem Statement: Alcohol abuse is one of the most critical problems facing society today (citation). The 12-step program has been purported to be the primary model for treatment of alcoholism (citation). Yet, to date, there has been little, if any, formal evaluation of the actual use and application of this program for those who are able to maintain abstinence. In order to provide the most effective and expeditious treatment for alcoholics, it is imperative that a study be done to determine to what extent those who have been successful in after care have utilized the 12-step program.

Introduction: Quote from Kaminer's *I'm Dysfunctional You're Dysfunctional*, questioning the efficacy, and discussing the overuse, of the 12-step program.

Purpose: The purpose of this study will be to evaluate a group of successful participants in Alcoholics Anonymous with respect to their degree of use of the 12 steps of Alcoholics Anonymous. Since the 12-step program is hailed as the paramount means of successfully treating those suffering from chemical dependency, it is imperative that those who have been successful in care conduct a study to ascertain the actual use of the program.

Theoretical Framework: The researcher is taking a postmodern constructivist view. In order to maintain sobriety the knowledge obtained in the treatment program is likely to be invented or "constructed" in the minds of people who have participated in the program. People create knowledge, ideas, and language, not because they are "true," but rather because they are useful. Perhaps those who are successful in care have constructed a modified theory based on the information they have received.

Research Question: To what extent is the 12-step program being used by those who have been successful in after care?

Significance: This study will be able to reach people who have not been reached before. The researcher will elaborate on his personal qualifications to obtain the desired information. If the study reveals that successful patients only practice part of the program then this information could aid counselors in seeking a more concentrated and abridged treatment regime, thus saving the patient, their family, and society time and money.

Background: 12-step program development; alcoholism as a disease.

Nature of the Study: A combination of ethnographic case study and evaluative study. The researcher believes that in order to elicit accurate information from this population, the investigator must have personal knowledge of this disease. The researcher plans to discover what the subjects believe or perceive they have experienced. The investigator further believes that nothing can be understood apart from the context within which it was experienced.

Literature/Research Review: After care, alcoholism, (5 yr. max.), 12-step program, alcohol as a disease, other programs for recovery and treatment of substance abuse; evaluation of other recovery programs. (Proposal, 10–20 pages, dissertation, 50–70 pages.)

Scope and Limitations: The subjects in this study are graduates of an alcoholic treatment center in Southern California and all reside in the Southern California area. The social conditions and anti-alcohol campaigns that are prevalent in this geographic region might not exist in other areas of the nation.

Methodology: The researcher is trying to determine how the 12-step program is actually being utilized. The population to be studied is alcoholics who have maintained sobriety for at least 1 year. The sample will come from graduates of an outpatient alcohol treatment center in Southern California, and will include approximately 25 men and 25 women, ages 20–60. Subjects will be selected with the help of personnel from the center and the willingness of patients to participate in the study. The researcher will use a questionnaire designed by experts in the area, and also conduct personal interviews. Questionnaire will make use of visual analog scale with multiple means of assessing the utilization of each step of the 12-step program. A panel of experts in the field will validate the instruments. Permission to do study will be obtained. The research will determine which of the 12 steps is most likely to be utilized by all, by gender and by age. Using descriptive statistics, the researcher will report on the step(s) that are most utilized by the group as a whole and by other criteria such as age and gender. The researcher will attempt to determine if there is a linear correlation between gender, ethnic group, age, occupation, and other factors and rankings of the 12 steps by the frequency of their use, using nonparametric statistics and multiple correlational hypothesis testing.

Definitions: sobriety, abstinence, 12-step program.

Social Impact of Study: Perhaps crime caused by alcoholism could be curtailed if there was a more effective treatment for alcoholics. In this day of instant everything, there is a constant search to condense and distill effective programs for the most expeditious implementation. If this study shows that successful patients do not utilize certain steps in the 12-step program, then an investigation of those steps might be studied in greater detail to determine their fruitfulness.

Proposal Outline/Blue Print/Prospectus for YOUR Study: _____

Problem Statement: (Write in full)

Introduction: (sketch)

Purpose: (sketch)

Significance: (sketch)

Limitations/Scope:

Theoretical Framework:

Background: (sketch)

Nature of the Study: (select type(s))

Definitions:

Literature Review: (areas to investigate)

Methodology:
    Research questions and/or hypotheses.

Population/Sample
    Instrument(s) (how to validate?)

Data:
How will you:
    Collect?
    Organize?
    Analyze?
    Interpret?
    Predict?

Social Impact: (give details)

Some Red Flags:

As you put your proposal together, keep in mind some things you **do not** want to include.

1. Do not use hyperbole—"everyone knows," "it is obvious," "this must be the case," "clearly."
2. Do not use clichés—"in this ever changing world."
3. Do not use gender specific terms: "For a person to be successful, HE must . . ."
4. Do not use a pronoun unless it is crystal clear to whom the pronoun is referring—"in their study they found."
5. Do not assume what you are trying to prove. If you are trying to determine if technology can help learning, do not start by assuming that technology helps learning.
6. Make certain that the headings always match the content.
7. If you plan to use articles that are not in peer-reviewed and refereed journals, make sure you obtain permission from your committee. Primary sources are preferred over secondary sources.
8. Most dissertations and formal research papers require the use of the third person voice. If this is the case, do not use statements with "I" or "me" or "we" or "our" in them.

Phase 3
The Feast [Your Dissertation/Research Paper]

Chapter 1 Appetizer [Introduction]

Chapter 2 Soup/Salad [Research Review]

Chapter 3/Chapter 4 Main Course [Methodology and Presentation]

Chapter 5 Dessert [Conclusions and Recommendations]

You are now ready to skillfully dish out a fastidiously prepared feast for your distinctive guests to delectably digest. As you carefully follow the directions in Phase 3 of your *Dissertation Cookbook*, and you present the research that you have done, you will be describing to your readers the importance and background of your problem and the way others have examined this problem. You will describe how you examined this problem and why you chose this method of inquiry. Finally, you will explain the fruits of your investigation and the recommendations that you want to make to others who will be contributing to the future solution or understanding of this problem.

Chapter 1 Appetizer

1/2 c.	Introduction	1 c.	Hypotheses/Research Questions
1/4 c.	Problem Statement	1/2 c.	Scope and Limitations
2 c.	Background	2 T.	Definitions
1/2 c.	Purpose		
1 c.	Significance		
1.5 c.	Nature of study		

Combine all ingredients carefully in a word processor. Simmer over all thoughts until mixture comes to a boil, stirring frequently with inspiration and ingenuity.

1/2 c. Introduction

The purpose of an Introduction Section is to capture the attention of the reader or set the stage for the courses to follow. An Introduction Section will acquaint the reader with the problem you are studying, the approach that you have chosen to study the problem, and your style of writing. It is the place where you begin to "dish" out your ideas and get your readers' "appetite whetted." An introduction gives the reader a PEAC (peek) at your study. It usually:

1. Puts your study in some perspective.
2. Establishes the need for your study.
3. Alerts the reader to what will follow.

3. Catches the attention and interest of the reader.

As suggested by the proportion, 1/2 c., the Introduction Section is usually brief (one or two pages at most). Below you will find some attention-getting ways to introduce the reader to your study, and, thus, begin your research paper.

___1. A dramatic illustration of the problem. Consider the worst-case scenario of the problem you are investigating or the best-case scenario if this problem did not exist.

___2. A quote from a passage that captures the problem. Share with the reader a study that calls attention to the problem you have researched or a quotation from a famous person that supports, or contradicts, your point of view.

___3. A narration describing how your interest in the problem was first piqued and how your convictions have changed since you have become aware of the problem and have conducted your study.

For Your Information and Education

Most research papers and, thus, dissertations are written in the past tense and in the third person. When relating an anecdotal story or a personal observation, it is usually proper etiquette to say "the researcher found" in lieu of "I find."

Cutting Board:

1. Which of the methods (1–3) above would you be most comfortable using in your introduction?_____.
2. Put yourself in the position of the reader. What about this study would capture your interest? Why is it important?
3. On a separate piece of paper, do a mind map of your introduction and attach it here:

Put a check next to each method you would consider using in the Introduction Section to your research paper.

___1. A dramatic illustration of the problem. Consider the worst-case scenario of the problem you are investigating or the best-case scenario if this problem did not exist.

___2. A quote from a passage that captures the problem. Share with the reader a study that calls attention to the problem you have researched or a quotation from a famous person that supports, or contradicts, your point of view.

___3. A narration describing how your interest in the problem was first piqued and how your convictions have changed since you have become aware of the problem and have conducted your study.

1/4 c. Problem Statement

The Problem Statement Section is the heart of the research paper. The mind seems to follow its own equivalent of Newton's law of inertia and becomes aroused to intense analysis only when some dilemma presents itself. Systematic thought, it seems, is driven by failure of established ideas, by a sense that something is wrong, by a belief that something needs closer attention, or by old ideas and methods which are no longer adequate.

The scope of your study, its ability to make a point, and the amount of research you need to do to make that point depend heavily on the initial specification of the problem or problems under investigation. The Problem Statement Section deals with the reality of the problem you are investigating, or the necessity of a program you are analyzing. The objective of a problem statement is:

1. To persuade your reader that the project is feasible, appropriate, and worthwhile, and
2. To capture and maintain your reader's attention.

The research methodology being employed often helps to dictate what the problem statement is. The following are drafts of potential problem statements that can be used in conjunction with the research methodologies specified for investigating the relationship between socioeconomic class and education. It is important that references and citations be included in the actual problem statement when appropriate.

Historical Research. Following the Civil War, teachers perceived children from the low socioeconomic strata of our society as "less intelligent." Such perceptions have had a disastrous effect on children in this group (example and reference to be supplied). It is imperative that a study be conducted to determine what about the Civil War has caused this problem to arise.

Evaluative Research. The government program Headstart seeks to afford children of low socioeconomic classes in our society an opportunity to increase the chances of their success in school by providing an enriched experiential background. It is important to determine if these lofty goals have been met. (*Note:* The implication is that if Headstart does what it purports to do, it should be continued and even expanded.)

Correlational Research. Children from the low socioeconomic strata of society may be denied proper education because teachers perceive them to be "less intelligent." It is imperative that a study be conducted to determine if there is a relationship between teachers' perceptions of students' ability and the quality of instruction administered.

Check to see if your Problem Statement, which you developed in Phase One, seeks an answer to one or more of the questions listed below.

My research determined or examined:

____1. What is wrong with society, or with one of its institutions, that has caused this problem or allowed this problem to exist?
____2. What has failed in society, which has caused this problem?
____3. What is missing in society that has allowed this problem to develop.
____4. What happened that has become interesting and important enough to study?
____5. What historical description of an event has become open to reexamination?
____6. A program that was in need of study, evaluation, or analysis.
____7. A need to develop a program that could contribute to society or one of its institutions.
____8. A need to analyze a current theory in light of new events.
____9. A relationship between the problem and a factor or factors that could be contributing to the problem.

Despite this lengthy description of how to develop the Problem Statement here, and in Phase One, the statement itself, when complete, should be relatively brief (one or two paragraphs). There is much to think about, but not a great deal to write. In fact, as long as it adequately conveys what you intend, the shorter the problem statement the better.

Cutting Board:

1. Which of the questions above does your study address?
2. What research methodology best describes your study? (Check back to Phase 1—What's cooking?)
3. In Phase 1 you created a problem statement prior to the formulation of your topic. Re-write that statement in the space below:

4. Make sure that you have stated the problem precisely and concisely. If that is not the case, re-write the problem sentence with your new insight: _____

2 c. Background

The Background Section often offsets the brevity of the Problem Statement Section. Here you will elaborate on why the problem you investigated is of pressing societal concern or theoretical interest. This is the place in your paper where you want to make your reader as interested in the problem as you are and help him/her understand the need for further elucidation of this problem.

Carefully read the statements below. Put a check next to the ones that apply to your research project and could potentially be used in the Background Section of your paper.

____1.   There are knowledgeable observers (political figures, theorists, newscasters, professionals in the field, etc.) who have attested to the importance of this problem.

____2.   There are statistics that have attested to the depth and spread of this problem.

____3.   The failure of certain aspects of society have made this problem compelling and in need of further examination.

____4.   There are theoretical issues that are in need of reexamination. This investigation identified these issues and determined the need for their reexamination.

____5.   There is a particular program or event in need of developing, investigating, or evaluating.

Cutting Board:

1. Which statements above pertain to your problem?
2. How will (did) you obtain information to support these statements? (Books, videos, articles, authorities?)

3. Give at least 3 reasons why the problem you chose is (was) important and valid to you, society, or some institution in society.
4. If applicable, give at least two concrete examples of the problem.
5. If applicable, what programs have addressed similar issues?
6. To what public statistics, political trends, theoretical controversy does your study relate?
7. What people, besides you, have been affected by this problem?
8. How was attention first called to the problem? (Name any key figure or figures who assisted in bringing this problem into focus.)

1/2 c. Purpose

The Purpose Statement Section deals with the reason that the study was conducted. It describes what you were trying to accomplish by doing your study. Stating the purpose of your study early will focus your reader's attention on the essentials of your project and what it was intended to accomplish. Thus, the reader will be better able to judge whether your approach was effective. In most proposals and dissertations, this is about three-fourths of a page. Here you will describe specifically what you intend to find out in your study and why this study is being (has been) conducted.

Put a check next to the phrases that could best be used to complete the statement:
The purpose of this research was to:

_____ 1. advance knowledge by understanding cause and effect;
_____ 2. provide new answers to old problems;
_____ 3. elucidate what makes the program under investigation successful or unsuccessful;
_____ 4. change a real situation and make it better;
_____ 5. interpret, evaluate, or analyze existing conditions;
_____ 6. determine to what extent certain factors contributed to the problem;
_____ 7. determine the need for a particular program or study;
_____ 8. describe a problem that has been given little attention up until this point, but could have a great impact on society;
_____ 9. understand why a particular condition exists and who is affected by this condition; and
_____ 10. elucidate what aspects of a program are successful and what aspects are not successful.

Cutting Board:

1. Which of the statements above apply to your study? _____
2. State briefly and precisely what your study intended to do about the problem you have specified by completing the following sentence: The purpose of this study was to _____

---

1 c. Significance

Just as the Background Section elaborates on the Problem Statement, the Significance Section elaborates on the Purpose Statement. In the Significance Section you will justify why you chose a particular type of research methodology.

Besides your personal desire and motivation to do research, your wish to obtain a degree, your need for a good grade, and your craving to get something published, there needs to be a more global reason for doing a worthwhile study. You should state who, besides yourself, your immediate family, and close friends cares that this research was done or not done. This should be about three-fourths of a page explaining why this is a unique approach and who will be thrilled (besides yourself, your family, and friends!) that this study is done. Here is where you tell us what type of contribution you will be making to your profession and to society at large.

The statements below are valid reasons for doing research. Put a check next to the ones that apply to your research project and can potentially be used in the Significance Section of your paper.

____1. This study was able to reach people who were not reached by other similar studies (i.e., a different population was studied).
____2. This study gave a different perspective on an established problem.
____3. This was an appropriate approach to this particular research problem although it had not been embraced before.
____4. There was an important benefit to doing the study this way so that there could be a better understanding of the problem.
____5. If this study was not done, some aspect of society would have been in danger.
____6. This was the first time the problem was examined in this vein.
____7. This study has the potential to effect social change.
____8. This program was needed to rectify certain wrongs in society.
____9. This study provided an objective measure of the success of a particular program.

Cutting Board:

1. Which statements above pertain to your study?
2. State in your own words why this study is important.
3. To whom is your study important, other than yourself?
4. How will society, or the understanding of a particular theory or program, benefit from your study?
5. How would you respond (in a nice way) to a person who says, "So what?" to your project?
6. How would you provide a persuasive rationale to the person who says, "so what"?
7. Write down several reasons why you chose to study the problem in this way. _____
    _____

1.5 c. Nature of Study

The Nature of the Study Section (about 2–3 pages) can also be called the research design section. This will be the place where the methodology you used is distinguished from other research methodologies that have been done, or could be done, to investigate this problem or program. It is the "blueprint" of your study, and places your study with similar types—case study, historical, correlational, evaluative, phenomenological, experimental, quasi-experimental. In this section you will elaborate on the methodology you have chosen, and justify why this is (was) such a great way to investigate this problem. If you use qualitative research methods you will probably need to do a little more explaining than if you choose (chose) a quantitative design. Provide details on your theoretical framework.

In Phase 1 we discussed different types of research methodologies. Refer to this section now and then answer the questions on the cutting board.

Cutting Board:

1. From what perspective did you view your problem: past, present, or future?
2. Which subset(s) of the past, present, or future perspective seemed to apply the most to your study (e.g., descriptive, correlational, grounded theory, action, heuristic)?
3. Within the perspective of one and two above which of the following do (did) you do:
   a. describe facts
   b. suggest causes
   c. analyze changes
   d. investigate relationships
   e. test causal hypotheses
   f. evaluate efficiency or effectiveness
   g. develop a program
   h. develop a theory
4. To summarize, complete the following statement: The methodology that I used in my study could best be classified as _____ study because I _____.
5. Name another type of methodology that could have been used to study the problem. Why did you reject this methodology?

---

1 c. Hypotheses/Research Questions

In the Hypotheses or Research Questions Section of your dissertation or formal research paper, you will elaborate on what you thought you would find prior to doing your study. A research hypothesis is a conjectural, declarative statement of the results you expect to find. Research hypotheses are sometimes referred to as working or substantive hypotheses. They are usually directional; that is, a researcher might believe something is more or less than a certain accepted notion or condition. Research questions tend to be more open and probative in nature and state the intent of the study.

There is a difference between a substantive hypothesis and a statistical hypothesis. The former speculates, somewhat informally, on what you assumed your study would reveal. The latter is a formal, testable conjecture that can be translated into mathematical symbols.

Example of a substantive hypothesis: Teachers who have integrated calculators into their own personal lives are more likely to use calculators in their classrooms than teachers who rarely use calculators.

Example of statistical hypotheses:

The null (no change) hypothesis is: H_0: There is no relationship between teachers using calculators in the classroom and using calculators every day.

$$r = 0$$

The alternative hypothesis: H_1: There is a relationship between teachers using calculators in the classroom and using calculators every day.

$$r \neq 0$$

Note: Statistical hypotheses (as discussed in Phase 2) usually come in pairs (the null or no change hypothesis, which contains =), and the alternative or opposite hypothesis, and are expressed symbolically. In statistical hypothesis testing you will either accept or reject (fail to accept) the null hypothesis.

In Chapter 1, only the substantive hypotheses or your expectations need to be expressed. (Statistical hypotheses belong in Chapter 3.)

Check the phrases below that best complete the following sentence: I believed that my study would disclose:

_____ 1. The extent to which this problem affects society or one of its institutions.
_____ 2. The true extent and/or nature of the problem.
_____ 3. A new interpretation to an old problem.
_____ 4. That the program (or treatment) evaluated was effective (or ineffective).
_____ 5. A significant relationship between the factors scrutinized and the problem under investigation.
_____ 6. A need to make a change in an attitude/condition.
_____ 7. Conditions that exist which contribute to the problem studied.
_____ 8. Specific conditions that exist as a result of the problem studied.
_____ 9. One program is more effective than another program.
_____10. There is a need for a particular study or program.

Cutting Board:

State as clearly and succinctly as possible what you expected the results of your study to show:

1/2 c. Scope and Limitations

In the Scope and Limitations Section (about 2–4 paragraphs) you will delineate special characteristics of your sample and the population from which it comes. For example, a study about education in California would not necessarily be applicable to other geographic regions. If the population is a sample by convenience and not randomized, it cannot be generally applied to a larger population, only suggested. If you are looking at one aspect, say achievement tests, then the information is only as good as the test itself. You can also give a philosophical framework to limit your study.

Note: When you are elaborating on the nature of your study and/or on the scope and limitations of your study you might wish to discuss your:

Ontology—How do you, the researcher, view reality: objectively? subjectively? a combination of the two?

Epistemology—What methodology(ies) will (did) you use to derive, elicit, and analyze data.

Theory—What interrelated constructs, definitions, and propositions will (did) you use to present a systematic view of the phenomenon you are studying? You need to specify relations among variables with the purpose of describing, explaining, and predicting the phenomenon you are studying.

2 T. Definitions

If you are using words in an unusual way, or you are employing words that have more than one definition, it is important that you set aside a section of your first chapter to define these terms. You may define a term operatively, that is, how the definition is being used in relation to your research. When possible quote an author who uses the terminology in this manner. For example: In this study, critical thinking is defined as a responsible appraisal that facilitates good judgment, relies upon criteria, is self-correcting, and is sensitive to context (Lipman, 1988, p. 3).

By understanding how you are using a term, the reader will be able to understand your research and appraise it objectively. Formal definitions consist of three parts: the term being defined, the general class to which the concept being defined belongs, and the specific characteristics that distinguish the term from other members of the class.

For example, a study on alternative learning might include: "For the purpose of this study, *distance education* refers to imparting knowledge where the learner and the facilitator are at different locations." (Simon, 2001)

Chapter 2 Soup/Salad [Research Review]

An acronym for what the Research/Literature Review chapter does is LEADS, for it "leads" the reader to the understanding of how your study fits into a larger picture of things, how others have dealt with and been affected by the problem, and why you chose to study the problem the way you did.

LEADS

1 c.   "L"ays the foundation for the study.

2 c.   "E"lucidates the problem.

1 c.   "A"nalyzes why your study is appropriate.

1 c.   "D"escribes why your study is capable of solving the problem.

1 c.   "S"hows studies similar to yours.

The Literature/Research Review chapter is one of the most important parts of your dissertation or research project. It describes in detail other studies that have dealt with the same or similar problems. It puts your research into a set with other studies and documents that have dealt with comparable issues. It gives you the knowledge to become an expert in the area that you are investigating. A thorough review of the literature also safeguards against undertaking a study that may have already been conducted, may not be feasible to do, or might not be of much value when set against what needs to be researched in a particular field.

Check back to Phase 1 in your *The Dissertation and Research Cookbook*'s Read Efficiently section to make sure that you are efficacious in your probing for information. Although there is no set rule on how many sources you need to consult for your dissertation, most chefs tend to review between 60 and 100 studies and/or programs that are related to their topic, and most Literature/Research Reviews constitute about one-fourth to one-half of the written research paper. These numbers will vary depending on:

1. How unique your study is.
2. How far back in time you choose to go.
3. How you define the related topics.

Just as there are restaurants that only serve soup and salad as a meal, the research/literature review itself could be your study.

In the Research/Literature Review chapter you will slowly illuminate how careful you were in preparing your exemplary "meal" and how familiar you are with the previous works that have been done in this area. As your readers "nibble" on the information you adeptly "dish out," you can unveil in this chapter why you chose your main course, why you decided to serve the meal the way you did, and why the utensils you chose were appropriate for this type of feast. Keep in mind that every reference should clearly relate to your study. Most universities (and research journals) require that most of the citations come from peer-reviewed journals that publish refereed articles. A refereed article is an article that has been carefully reviewed and scrutinized by scholars or experts in the research topic of the article who are not members of the editorial staff or board. In many cases one or more external readers have subjected the article to a blind review process. Walden University has prepared a guide to assist you in finding acceptable scholarly material at *http://www.lib.waldenu.edu/judge.html.*

Evaluating a source can begin even before you have the source in hand. You can initially appraise a source by first examining the bibliographic citation—a written description of a book, journal article, essay, or some other published material. Bibliographic citations characteristically have three main components: author, title, and publication information. These components can help you determine the usefulness of the source for your paper.

Recipe for Appraising an Author

1. What are the author's credentials—educational background, past writings, or experience—in this area? Is the book or article written on a topic in the author's area of expertise?
2. Have you seen the author's name cited in other sources or bibliographies? Other scholars cite respected authors frequently. For this reason, always note those names that appear in many different sources.
3. Is the author associated with an institution or organization? What are the basic values or goals of the organization or institution?

Check the Date of Publication

1. When was the source published? This date is often located on the face of the title page below the name of the publisher. If it is not there, look for the copyright date on the reverse of the title page. On Web pages, the date of the last revision is usually at the bottom of the home page, sometimes every page.
2. Is the source current or out-of-date for your topic? Topic areas of continuing and rapid development, such as technology, demand more current information. On the other hand, topics in the arts often require material that was written many years ago.

Check the Edition or Revision

Is this a first edition of this publication? Further editions indicate a source has been revised and updated to reflect changes in knowledge, rectify omissions, and harmonize with its intended readers' needs. Also, many printings or editions may indicate that the work has become a standard source in the area and is reliable.

Check the Publisher

If a university press publishes the source, it is likely to be scholarly. Although the fact that the publisher is reputable does not necessarily guarantee quality, it does show that the publisher may have high regard for the source being published.

Check the Title of Journal

Is this a scholarly or a popular journal? This distinction is important because it indicates different levels of complexity in conveying ideas. If you need help in determining the type of journal, you may wish to check your journal title in the latest edition of *Katz's Magazines for Libraries* (Uri's Ref Z 6941 .K21 1995) for a brief evaluative description.

Keyword searching is a powerful and flexible way to find books, periodicals, and other materials. A keyword search looks for any word or combination of words in the author, title, and subject fields of databases. Keyword searches use connectors to search for two or more words in specific ways. The three most useful connectors are AND, OR, and ADJ. AND specifies that both words must appear somewhere in the document, thus NARROWING your search. OR specifies that either word may appear in the record. ADJ specifies that the words must be adjacent and in the same order, thus guaranteeing that the words are searched AS A PHRASE. This can also be accomplished using quotation marks: "child psychology" works the same as child ADJ psychology.

The questions below can be used to describe and assess the merits of previous studies, and could be included when writing the Literature/Research Review in your research paper. It is unlikely that any one study will provide the answers to all these questions, but the questions can serve as a guideline for critical reviews.

1. What was done? Was it effective?
2. When did this take place? What was the accepted belief at this time?
3. Where did this study or event take place?
4. Who was involved?
5. What methodologies were used?
6. What were the limitations? How were these limitations addressed?
7. What type of instruments were used?
8. What was the sample and population studied?
9. What did this add to the knowledge or solution of the problem?
10. What recommendations were made?
11. Who was affected by this study or program?
12. What are the similarities between this study and your study?
13. Was this an appropriate means of dealing with the problem?

According to Simpson (1989), a literature review functions as a means of conceptualizing, justifying, implementing, and interpreting a research investigation. Without a literature review it is impossible for others to ascertain the significance of your study and how it will contribute to the knowledge base of a field.

Cutting Board:

1. As you examine articles, textbooks, speeches, video presentations, web pages, documentaries, etc., that are related to your topic and the problem you are investigating, determine which of the questions delineated were addressed and which should have been addressed. Elaborate on other issues that the materials dealt with related to your problem or topic.
2. In the space below, write down key words that are closely related to your research.
3. Remember to write down the following information, if applicable, after you have examined a source: Author, publisher, city of publisher, copyright date, title, page number, name of periodical, date, volume number, quotes you plan to use, page number of quotes. An excellent place to help you evaluate a source can be found at *http://trochim.human.cornell.edu/kb/kbhome.htm*

Chapter 3 One-Half Main Course [Methodology—What did you do?]

Congratulations! Now that you have reached this point in your *The Dissertation and Research Cookbook,* you are ready to put together many of the ingredients that you have carefully amassed in Phases 1 and 2 and create a splendid main course.

The cutting board activity that follows can be used to prepare a delicious and nutritious Chapter 3 in a jiffy. For your proposal this usually is 4–8 pages; in your dissertation it is usually 10–25 pages; in qualitative studies it is usually 25–50 pages.

Cutting Board:

From Phase 2 obtain the following information:

1. What population did you study?
2. How did you choose your sample? (What criteria did you use?) How did you contact your subjects or obtain the documentation you needed?
3. How large was your "*n*" (How large was your sample?)
4. Classify your study. (Look at the What's Cooking Section and inform the reader about the type of research methodology you used.)
5. Why did you chose this type of methodology?
6. What type of instrument(s) did you use?
7. Why did you choose these types of instruments?
8. Explain any means you had of knowing the instruments were valid and reliable.
9. Describe (in great detail) the procedure you used to administer your instruments and obtain your data.
10. Who else was involved in this aspect of the study?

11. Explain any special things you needed to do to see that the information you sought after was obtained and reliable.
12. If you did a pilot study, what information did you obtain from that inquiry?
13. What were your statistical hypotheses?
14. Describe how you tested your hypotheses.
15. If you used a statistical package on a computer. What program was it? Why did you choose it?
16. Describe any problems or snags that you encountered while obtaining your data.

Each sub-section of Chapter 3 should be highlighted in some way. You want to convince the reader that you have (had) a well-thought-out plan to collect, organize, analyze, and interpret data. You must convince the reader that you can (did) achieve the purpose of your study.

It is usually easier to use an instrument that has an established "cooking" record rather than to create your own. This means that it has probably already been shown to be both valid and reliable. However, if you have created your own instrument for data collection, then you must describe what you have done to show that it is valid (does what it purports to do) and how you know it is reliable (consistent). Panels of experts, pilot studies, and content analysis can help in this respect.

Stir and fry all the ingredients together and arrange them in a pleasing and delectable manner and you will have one-half of your main course and Chapter 3 of your dissertation complete! Savor the taste.

Chapter 4 The Other Half of the Main Course [Presentation and Analysis of Data]

Here is where you provide the "punch line" or tell the reader what you discovered from your study. You have already made the preliminary preparation for this Chapter in Phase 2 of your *The Dissertation and Research Cookbook.* You can use that information to guide you through the writing of Chapter 4 of your dissertation or reporting the analysis of data.

The Presentation and Analysis chapter of your dissertation usually contains many of the "garnishes" listed below. Check each "ingredient" that you plan to include. (Once you have successfully incorporated a particular component into the body of your paper, acknowledge that accomplishment by highlighting that task with a colorful pen.)

_____1. A detailed description of the data uncovered (include means, percentages, standard deviations, t or z values, rho values, chi square values, p values, alpha values, ANOVA, etc.).

_____2. Tables and graphs depicting your data.

_____3. The results of your hypothesis testing.

_____4. The statistical significance of your findings.

_____5. The answer to every research question you posed.

_____6. A summary of any interviews that you conducted.

_____7. Any observations that you, or a research assistant, made in relation to the problem.

_____8. If you used surveys or tests, an explanation of how each item was weighted and how it was used to help you arrive at your conclusions.

The more conventional your analysis, the less detail you may need to provide, because the meaning of what you are doing will be more obvious to your reader. On the other hand, if you are doing something unusual you should build the case for its legitimacy here.

Chapter 5 Dessert [Conclusions, Implications, and Recommendations]

Kudos, cheers, and compliments to the "chef." It is now time to relax and savor the final moments of your eloquent banquet. Here is the time where you can editorialize about your study and advise future cooks on how to cultivate similar feasts.

Put a check next to each item that you plan to serve for dessert.

____ 1. A summary of what your study found.
____ 2. An editorial on what your findings mean to the population you studied.
____ 3. A discourse on how your findings will affect society in general.
____ 4. Suggestions to others on how to serve a similar feast at a future banquet.
____ 5. Advice on what can be done to solve the problem in light of your findings.
____ 6. A list of things that need closer examination in light of your findings.
____ 7. An opinion on how effective the program, product, or treatment you studied was in meeting its goals and what changes you would like to see made in the future.
____ 8. Suggestions on how the program, theory, treatment, or model that you developed will, or could, be implemented while speculating on the anticipated results.
____ 9. What you might have done differently with the benefit of hindsight.
____10. What further study will most likely need to be done now that yours is complete?
____11. Who needs to pay attention to the results of your study and how will that information be given to them?
____12. How will the information you obtained affect your sample? population? society?
____13. What surprises (if any) did you find in your research?
____14. What has your study done to add to the understanding of the larger problem?
____15. What studies were most in accord with yours?
____16. What studies were most in opposition to yours?
____17. What questions did your study raise?
____18. What final conclusions, if any, can be drawn from your study?

Make sure that you quote **your study** when supporting information in your results, conclusions, or summary.

Abstract [Menu]

Most research papers are preceded by an abstract, a brief summary of the research. This serves as a "menu" for your feast. When putting together your abstract make sure you include:

1. a statement of the problem you have investigated.
2. a brief description of the research method and design.
3. major findings and their significance.
4. conclusions and recommendations.

A reader should be able to decide from the abstract whether to read the entire dissertation. Since it is not part of the dissertation it should neither be numbered nor counted as a page. To fulfill the requirement that the doctoral dissertation be available to other scholars, you or your graduate school generally sends a copy of the abstract to University Microfilms, which will print your abstract in *Dissertation Abstracts International* (DAI). Abstracts published in DAI are limited to a maximum of 350 words.

As for the form and style:

(2.5 cm)

Abstract [or ABSTRACT]

(double space)
Title

(double space)
by

(double space)

Author
(double space)
Text (double spaced and about 1.5 pages)

Acknowledgments

You can now celebrate the birth of an excellent contribution to society and a remarkable repast. You probably want to write "thank you cards" by adding an acknowledgments page after the table of contents to show your appreciation to everyone who helped you create this feast.

Thank you for allowing *The Dissertation and Research Cookbook* to accompany you through this culinary delight. If you know a person who is ABD (All But Dissertation) or someone in need of a guide to successfully complete a research paper, please fill out the form on the last page and we will see that they receive their own copy of *The Dissertation and Research Cookbook*.

Bon Appetit!

Suggested Readings

Sax, G. (1979). *Fundamentals of educational research*. New Jersey: Prentice Hall.

This work is a practical guide to graduate level research in education. It shows how to select a research project, how to conduct the research, and how to interpret the research. It carries the reader from analysis to presentation of research.

Gilovich, T. (1991). *How we know what isn't so: The fallibility of human reason in everyday life*. New York: Free Press, A Division of Macmillan, Inc.

Gilovich explains in detail the truth to Artemus Ward's famous expression, "It ain't so much the things we don't know that get us in trouble. It's the things we know that just ain't so." He examines how questionable and erroneous beliefs are formed, and how they are maintained. Despite popular opinion, people do not hold questionable beliefs simply because they have not been exposed to the relevant evidence, or because they are unintelligent or gullible. Many questionable and erroneous beliefs have purely cognitive origins, and can be traced to imperfections in our capacity to process information and draw conclusions. They are not the products of irrationality, but of flawed rationality.

Slavin, R. (1984). *Research methods in education: A practical guide.* New Jersey: Prentice Hall.

This text is primarily designed to serve as a basic resource for a course on research methods of education, but it can also be used by anyone who expects to conduct social science research. Its intent is to show how to use research designs and procedures to get the best possible answers to the best possible questions. It discusses research design issues in the light of the limitations and realities of institutional settings.

Fink, A., & Kosekoff, J. (1985). *How to conduct surveys: A step-by-step guide.* Beverly Hills, CA: Sage Publications.

The purpose of this guide is to help the reader organize a rigorous survey and evaluate the credibility of existing surveys. Its aim is for simplicity rather than embellishment.

Turney, B., & Robb, G. (1971). *Research in education: An introduction.* Hinsdale, IL: The Dryden Press Inc.

This book deals with issues such as "What constitutes research? What is the scientific approach to research? How do you select and evaluate a research problem?" It offers advice on using the library in educational research and discusses in detail techniques and tools of the educational researcher.

Bertrand, A., & Cebula, J. P. (1980). *Tests, measurement and evaluation: A developmental approach.* Menlo Park, CA: Addison Wesley Co.

The testing movement in America has come under severe criticism in recent years by those who claim that there is too much emphasis on "standardized" instruments to measure intelligence and achievement. Some have even referred to such tests as "dehumanizing" and inaccurate assessments of individual differences.

This book takes the view that tests in and of themselves are not dangerous, but when used properly can provide the classroom teacher with a helpful set of assessment tools. It takes a developmental approach to learning and growth, emphasizing the need to understand each developmental stage of physical, cognitive and personal growth and how each stage dramatically affects the others throughout a child's life.

Fowler, F. J., Jr. (1988). *Survey research methods.* Newbury Park, CA: Sage Publications.

The main purpose of this text is to produce a comprehensive summary of current knowledge about sources of error in surveys, in particular, the emphasis on minimizing nonsampling errors through question design. It also includes a chapter coding and filing preparation to reflect the current importance of computer-assisted telephone interviewing (CATI) and direct data entry systems.

Bradburn, N., & Sudman, S. (1979). *Improving interview methods and questionnaire design.* San Francisco: Jossey-Bass, Inc.

This book presents the results of a research program on "response effects" in surveys conducted by the National Opinion Research Center (NORC), and concentrates on research areas most in need of empirical work. The three major variables that affect response rate delineated by the authors are the task itself, the characteristics of the interviewer, and the characteristics of the respondents. The text not only attempts to describe and measure the response effects that are occurring but also to suggest the procedures that yield the most accurate reporting.

Borg, W. R. (1987). *Applying educational research.* New York: Longman, Inc.

The main goal of this book is to make the reader an intelligent consumer of educational research. This involves the ability to locate research relevant to a given problem, evaluate such research, and interpret the research findings.

The author feels that the useful information that has emerged from educational research is difficult to locate and even more difficult to interpret and to relate to the practical problems that teachers and school administrators must address. They quote a study by Reys and Yeager (1974) that reported that 87.5% of in-service teachers never read research articles. He believes this trend must be reversed if teaching is to become a true profession.

Reason, P., & Rowan, J. *Human inquiry: A sourcebook.* New York, John Wiley and Sons.

According to the authors, there has been much criticism of orthodox research but few have suggested alternatives. This book covers the philosophy, methodology, and practice of research, which is collaborative and experiential. They believe that social science research should be with people instead of on people.

Triola, M. (1999). *Elementary statistics* (7th ed.) Menlo Park, CA: Benjamin Cummings Co.

A user-friendly text that does not require a strong mathematics background to be understood. It is an interesting and readable source to familiarize the reader with statistics and statistical methods, and it is even written with a sense of humor.

Gall, M., Borg, W., & Call, J. (1996). *Educational research* (6th ed.).

This is one of the most comprehensive introductions to educational research. There is an excellent balance between both quantitative and qualitative research methods.

References

Bertrand, A., & Cebula. J. P. (1980). *Tests, measurement and evaluation.* Menlo Park, CA: Addison Wesley Co.

Bogdan , R. C., & Biklen, S. K. (1992). *Introduction to qualitative research for education: An introduction to theory and methods.* Boston, MA: Allyn and Bacon.

Borg, W. R. (1987). *Applying educational research.* New York: Longman, Inc.

Bradburn, N., Sudman, S., and associates (1979). Improving Interview Methods and Questionnaire Design. Jossey-Bass, Inc., San Francisco, CA.

Burns, J. M. (1989). *The American experiment.* New York: Knopf.

Burns, N. & Grove K. (1993). *The practice of nursing research: Conduct, critique and utilization* (2nd ed.). Philadelphia, PA: Saunders.

Cheek (1992). *Vertification: Logic.* Dulles, VA: Brassey's.

Clements, Copeland, & Loftus (1990). *Mathematical modeling; a case study approach.* Cambridge, MA: Cambridge University Press.

Cormack, D. (1991). *Team spirit motivation and commitment team leadership and membership, team evaluation.* Grand Rapids, MI: Pyranee Books.

Creswell, J. (1994). Research Design: Qualitative & Quantiative Approaches. Thousand Oaks: Sage Publications.

Crossen, Cynthia (1995). *The Tainted Truth: The manipulation of fact in America.* Simon & Schuster: New York.

Dalkey, N. (1984) *The Delphi Method: An experimental study of group opinion.* Thousand Oaks: Sage Publications.

Fink, A., & Kosekoff, J. (1985). *How to conduct surveys: A step-by-step guide.* Beverly Hills, CA: Sage Publications.

Fowler, F. J., Jr. (1988). *Survey research methods.* Newbury Park, CA: Sage Publications.

Gilovitch, T. (1991). *How what we know isn't so.* New York: Free Press, A Division of Macmillan, Inc.

Glaser, B., & Strauss, A. (1967). *The discovery of grounded theory.* Chicago: Aldine Publishing Co.

Goetz, J. P., & LeCompte, M. D. (1984). *Ethnography and qualitative design in educational research.* San Diego, CA: Academic Press.

Goldstein, M., & Goldstein, N. (1985). *The experience of science: An interdisciplinary approach.* New York: Plenum Press.

Guba, E., & Lincoln, Y. S. (1986). *Effective evaluation.* San Francisco: Jossey-Bass

Guba, E. & Lincoln, Y. S. (1989). *Fourth generation evaluation.* San Francisco: Jossey-Bass.

Guba, E. (1990). *The paradigm dialogue.* Newbury, CA: Sage.

Hanau (1975) *The study game: How to play and win with "statement-pie."* New York: Barnes & Noble Books.

Hitchcock & Hughes. (1995). *Research and the teacher: A qualitative introduction to school based research.* London: Routledge.

Koehler, K. J., & Larntz, K. (1980). An empirical investigation of goodness-of-fit statistics for sparse multinomials. *Journal of the American Statistical Association 75,* 336–344.

Lewin, K. (1946). Group Decision and Social Change. In Merriam, S. B., & Simpson, E. L. *A guide to research for educators and trainers of adults.* Malabar, FL: Krieger Publishing Company.

Lichtman, M., & Taylor, S. I. (1993). *The first book of Lotus 1-2-3* (3rd ed.). Indianapolis, IN: Sams.

Lindstone, J. & Turoff, M. (1975). *The Delphi method, techniques and applications.* London: Addison-Wesley Publishing.

Mills-Novoa, B. (1997). *The use of qualitative methods in the evaluation* (2nd ed.). Alexandria, VA: Capitol Publications.

Mitroff, & Kilman, R. H. (1978). *Methodological approaches to social science.* San Francisco: Jossey-Bass.

Morse, J. M. (1989). *Qualitative nursing research: A contemporary dialogue.* Sandy, UT: Aspen Systems Corp.

Moustakis, C. (1961). Heuristic research. In J. Bugental (ed.), *Challenges of humanistic psychology.* New York: McGraw-Hill.

Munhall, K. G. & Stetson, R. H. (1989). *R. H. Stetson's motor phonetics* (2nd ed.). New York: Little, Brown.

Polit, D., & Hungler, B. (1991). *Nursing research: Principals and methods* (2nd ed.). Philadelphia, PA: Lippincott.

Reason, P., & Rowan, J. (1987). *A sourcebook of new paradigm research.* New York: Longman, Inc.

Salkind, N.J. (1985). *Theories of human development* (2nd ed.). New York: Wiley.

Simpson, M. (1989). *A guide to research for educators and trainers of adults.* Malabar, FL: Krieger Publishing Co.

Simon, M. (2000). In White and Waite: *The online teaching guide.* Boston: Allyn and Bacon.

Sproull, N. (1995). *Handbook of research methods: A guide for practitioners in the social sciences.* Metchen, NJ: The Scarecrow Press.

Stringer, E. T. (1996). *Action research; a handbook for practitioners.* Thousand Oaks, CA: Sage Publications.

Suskie, L. (1996). *Questionnaire survey research: What works* (2nd ed.). Washington, DC: Assn. for International Research.

Taylor R., & Meinhardt, R. (1985, April). Defining computer information needs for small business: A delphi method. *Journal of Small Business Management, 23,* p. 3.

Triola, M. (1999). *Elementary statistics* (7th ed.). Chicago: Addison-Wesley.

Turney, B. & Robb, G. (1971). *Research in education: An introduction.* Hinsdale, Illinois, The Dryden Press, Inc.

Vygotsky, L. S. (1978). *Mind in society: The development of higher psychological processes* (M. Cole, V. John-Steiner, S. Scribner, & E. Souberman, Eds.). Cambridge, MA: Harvard University Press.

Wolfowitz, J. & A. Wald (1952) *Nonparametric statistics. Annals of Mathematics Statistics,* p. 23.

Wood & Brink (1989). *Principles of string theory.* New York: Plenum Press.

Yager, J. (1991). *Business protocol: How to survive and succeed in business.* New York: Wiley.

Appendix

The Standardized Normal Distribution

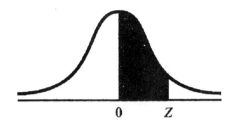

0   Z

Entry represents area under the standardized normal distribution from the mean to Z

Z	.00	.01	.02	.03	.04	.05	.06	.07	.08	.09
0.0	.0000	.0040	.0080	.0120	.0160	.0199	.0239	.0279	.0319	.0359
0.1	.0398	.0438	.0478	.0517	.0557	.0596	.0636	.0675	.0714	.0753
0.2	.0793	.0832	.0871	.0910	.0948	.0987	.1026	.1064	.1103	.1141
0.3	.1179	.1217	.1255	.1293	.1331	.1368	.1406	.1443	.1480	.1517
0.4	.1554	.1591	.1628	.1664	.1700	.1736	.1772	.1808	.1844	.1879
0.5	.1915	.1950	.1985	.2019	.2054	.2088	.2123	.2157	.2190	.2224
0.6	.2257	.2291	.2324	.2357	.2389	.2422	.2454	.2486	.2518	.2549
0.7	.2580	.2612	.2642	.2673	.2704	.2734	.2764	.2794	.2823	.2852
0.8	.2881	.2910	.2939	.2967	.2995	.3023	.3051	.3078	.3106	.3133
0.9	.3159	.3186	.3212	.3238	.3264	.3289	.3315	.3340	.3365	.3389
1.0	.3413	.3438	.3461	.3485	.3508	.3531	.3554	.3577	.3599	.3621
1.1	.3643	.3665	.3686	.3708	.3729	.3749	.3770	.3790	.3810	.3830
1.2	.3849	.3869	.3888	.3907	.3925	.3944	.3962	.3980	.3997	.4015
1.3	.4032	.4049	.4066	.4082	.4099	.4115	.4131	.4147	.4162	.4177
1.4	.4192	.4207	.4222	.4236	.4251	.4265	.4279	.4292	.4306	.4319
1.5	.4332	.4345	.4357	.4370	.4382	.4394	.4406	.4418	.4429	.4441
1.6	.4452	.4463	.4474	.4484	.4495	.4505	.4515	.4525	.4535	.4545
1.7	.4554	.4564	.4573	.4582	.4591	.4599	.4608	.4616	.4625	.4633
1.8	.4641	.4649	.4656	.4664	.4671	.4678	.4686	.4693	.4699	.4706
1.9	.4713	.4719	.4726	.4732	.4738	.4744	.4750	.4756	.4761	.4767
2.0	.4772	.4778	.4783	.4788	.4793	.4798	.4803	.4808	.4812	.4817
2.1	.4821	.4826	.4830	.4834	.4838	.4842	.4846	.4850	.4854	.4857
2.2	.4861	.4864	.4868	.4871	.4875	.4878	.4881	.4884	.4887	.4890
2.3	.4893	.4896	.4898	.4901	.4904	.4906	.4909	.4911	.4913	.4916
2.4	.4918	.4920	.4922	.4925	.4927	.4929	.4931	.4932	.4934	.4936
2.5	.4938	.4940	.4941	.4943	.4945	.4946	.4948	.4949	.4951	.4952
2.6	.4953	.4955	.4956	.4957	.4959	.4960	.4961	.4962	.4963	.4964
2.7	.4965	.4966	.4967	.4968	.4969	.4970	.4971	.4972	.4973	.4974
2.8	.4974	.4975	.4976	.4977	.4977	.4978	.4979	.4979	.4980	.4981
2.9	.4981	.4982	.4982	.4983	.4984	.4984	.4985	.4985	.4986	.4986
3.0	.49865	.49869	.49874	.49878	.49882	.49886	.49889	.49893	.49897	.49900
3.1	.49903	.49906	.49910	.49913	.49916	.49918	.49921	.49924	.49926	.49929
3.2	.49931	.49934	.49936	.49938	.49940	.49942	.49944	.49946	.49948	.49950
3.3	.49952	.49953	.49955	.49957	.49958	.49960	.49961	.49962	.49964	.49965
3.4	.49966	.49968	.49969	.49970	.49971	.49972	.49973	.49974	.49975	.49976
3.5	.49977	.49978	.49978	.49979	.49980	.49981	.49981	.49982	.49983	.49983
3.6	.49984	.49985	.49985	.49986	.49986	.49987	.49987	.49988	.49988	.49989
3.7	.49989	.49990	.49990	.49990	.49991	.49991	.49992	.49992	.49992	.49992
3.8	.49993	.49993	.49993	.49994	.49994	.49994	.49994	.49995	.49995	.49995
3.9	.49995	.49995	.49996	.49996	.49996	.49996	.49996	.49996	.49997	.49997

From *Statistics for Managers Using Microsoft Excel* by Levine-Berenson. © 1999. Reprinted by permission of Pearson Education, Inc., Upper Saddle River, NJ 07458.

Critical Values of t

For particular number of degrees of freedom,
entry represents the critical value of t
corresponding to a specified upper tail area (α)

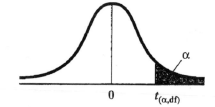

Degrees of Freedom	Upper Tail Areas					
	.25	.10	.05	.025	.01	.005
1	1.0000	3.0777	6.3138	12.7062	31.8207	63.6574
2	0.8165	1.8856	2.9200	4.3027	6.9646	9.9248
3	0.7649	1.6377	2.3534	3.1824	4.5407	5.8409
4	0.7407	1.5332	2.1318	2.7764	3.7469	4.6041
5	0.7267	1.4759	2.0150	2.5706	3.3649	4.0322
6	0.7176	1.4398	1.9432	2.4469	3.1427	3.7074
7	0.7111	1.4149	1.8946	2.3646	2.9980	3.4995
8	0.7064	1.3968	1.8595	2.3060	2.8965	3.3554
9	0.7027	1.3830	1.8331	2.2622	2.8214	3.2498
10	0.6998	1.3722	1.8125	2.2281	2.7638	3.1693
11	0.6974	1.3634	1.7959	2.2010	2.7181	3.1058
12	0.6955	1.3562	1.7823	2.1788	2.6810	3.0545
13	0.6938	1.3502	1.7709	2.1604	2.6503	3.0123
14	0.6924	1.3450	1.7613	2.1448	2.6245	2.9768
15	0.6912	1.3406	1.7531	2.1315	2.6025	2.9467
16	0.6901	1.3368	1.7459	2.1199	2.5835	2.9208
17	0.6892	1.3334	1.7396	2.1098	2.5669	2.8982
18	0.6884	1.3304	1.7341	2.1009	2.5524	2.8784
19	0.6876	1.3277	1.7291	2.0930	2.5395	2.8609
20	0.6870	1.3253	1.7247	2.0860	2.5280	2.8453
21	0.6864	1.3232	1.7207	2.0796	2.5177	2.8314
22	0.6858	1.3212	1.7171	2.0739	2.5083	2.8188
23	0.6853	1.3195	1.7139	2.0687	2.4999	2.8073
24	0.6848	1.3178	1.7109	2.0639	2.4922	2.7969
25	0.6844	1.3163	1.7081	2.0595	2.4851	2.7874
26	0.6840	1.3150	1.7056	2.0555	2.4786	2.7787
27	0.6837	1.3137	1.7033	2.0518	2.4727	2.7707
28	0.6834	1.3125	1.7011	2.0484	2.4671	2.7633
29	0.6830	1.3114	1.6991	2.0452	2.4620	2.7564
30	0.6828	1.3104	1.6973	2.0423	2.4573	2.7500
31	0.6825	1.3095	1.6955	2.0395	2.4528	2.7440
32	0.6822	1.3086	1.6939	2.0369	2.4487	2.7385
33	0.6820	1.3077	1.6924	2.0345	2.4448	2.7333
34	0.6818	1.3070	1.6909	2.0322	2.4411	2.7284
35	0.6816	1.3062	1.6896	2.0301	2.4377	2.7238
36	0.6814	1.3055	1.6883	2.0281	2.4345	2.7195
37	0.6812	1.3049	1.6871	2.0262	2.4314	2.7154
38	0.6810	1.3042	1.6860	2.0244	2.4286	2.7116
39	0.6808	1.3036	1.6849	2.0227	2.4258	2.7079
40	0.6807	1.3031	1.6839	2.0211	2.4233	2.7045
41	0.6805	1.3025	1.6829	2.0195	2.4208	2.7012
42	0.6804	1.3020	1.6820	2.0181	2.4185	2.6981
43	0.6802	1.3016	1.6811	2.0167	2.4163	2.6951
44	0.6801	1.3011	1.6802	2.0154	2.4141	2.6923
45	0.6800	1.3006	1.6794	2.0141	2.4121	2.6896
46	0.6799	1.3002	1.6787	2.0129	2.4102	2.6870
47	0.6797	1.2998	1.6779	2.0117	2.4083	2.6846
48	0.6796	1.2994	1.6772	2.0106	2.4066	2.6822
49	0.6795	1.2991	1.6766	2.0096	2.4049	2.6800
50	0.6794	1.2987	1.6759	2.0086	2.4033	2.6778

continued

Critical Values of t (continued)

Degrees of Freedom	Upper Tail Areas					
	.25	.10	.05	.025	.01	.005
51	0.6793	1.2984	1.6753	2.0076	2.4017	2.6757
52	0.6792	1.2980	1.6747	2.0066	2.4002	2.6737
53	0.6791	1.2977	1.6741	2.0057	2.3988	2.6718
54	0.6791	1.2974	1.6736	2.0049	2.3974	2.6700
55	0.6790	1.2971	1.6730	2.0040	2.3961	2.6682
56	0.6789	1.2969	1.6725	2.0032	2.3948	2.6665
57	0.6788	1.2966	1.6720	2.0025	2.3936	2.6649
58	0.6787	1.2963	1.6716	2.0017	2.3924	2.6633
59	0.6787	1.2961	1.6711	2.0010	2.3912	2.6618
60	0.6786	1.2958	1.6706	2.0003	2.3901	2.6603
61	0.6785	1.2956	1.6702	1.9996	2.3890	2.6589
62	0.6785	1.2954	1.6698	1.9990	2.3880	2.6575
63	0.6784	1.2951	1.6694	1.9983	2.3870	2.6561
64	0.6783	1.2949	1.6690	1.9977	2.3860	2.6549
65	0.6783	1.2947	1.6686	1.9971	2.3851	2.6536
66	0.6782	1.2945	1.6683	1.9966	2.3842	2.6524
67	0.6782	1.2943	1.6679	1.9960	2.3833	2.6512
68	0.6781	1.2941	1.6676	1.9955	2.3824	2.6501
69	0.6781	1.2939	1.6672	1.9949	2.3816	2.6490
70	0.6780	1.2938	1.6669	1.9944	2.3808	2.6479
71	0.6780	1.2936	1.6666	1.9939	2.3800	2.6469
72	0.6779	1.2934	1.6663	1.9935	2.3793	2.6459
73	0.6779	1.2933	1.6660	1.9930	2.3785	2.6449
74	0.6778	1.4931	1.6657	1.9925	2.3778	2.6439
75	0.6778	1.2929	1.6654	1.9921	2.3771	2.6430
76	0.6777	1.2928	1.6652	1.9917	2.3764	2.6421
77	0.6777	1.2926	1.6649	1.9913	2.3758	2.6412
78	0.6776	1.2925	1.6646	1.9908	2.3751	2.6403
79	0.6776	1.2924	1.6644	1.9905	2.3745	2.6395
80	0.6776	1.2922	1.6641	1.9901	2.3739	2.6387
81	0.6775	1.2921	1.6639	1.9897	2.3733	2.6379
82	0.6775	1.2920	1.6636	1.9893	2.3727	2.6371
83	0.6775	1.2918	1.6634	1.9890	2.3721	2.6364
84	0.6774	1.2917	1.6632	1.9886	2.3716	2.6356
85	0.6774	1.2916	1.6630	1.9883	2.3710	2.6349
86	0.6774	1.2915	1.6628	1.9879	2.3705	2.6342
87	0.6773	1.2914	1.6626	1.9876	2.3700	2.6335
88	0.6773	1.2912	1.6624	1.9873	2.3695	2.6329
89	0.6773	1.2911	1.6622	1.9870	2.3690	2.6322
90	0.6772	1.2910	1.6620	1.9867	2.3685	2.6316
91	0.6772	1.2909	1.6618	1.9864	2.3680	2.6309
92	0.6772	1.2908	1.6616	1.9861	2.3676	2.6303
93	0.6771	1.2907	1.6614	1.9858	2.3671	2.6297
94	0.6771	1.2906	1.6612	1.9855	2.3667	2.6291
95	0.6771	1.2905	1.6611	1.9853	2.3662	2.6286
96	0.6771	1.2904	1.6609	1.9850	2.3658	2.6280
97	0.6770	1.2903	1.6607	1.9847	2.3654	2.6275
98	0.6770	1.2902	1.6606	1.9845	2.3650	2.6269
99	0.6770	1.2902	1.6604	1.9842	2.3646	2.6264
100	0.6770	1.2901	1.6602	1.9840	2.3642	2.6259
110	0.6767	1.2893	1.6588	1.9818	2.3607	2.6213
120	0.6765	1.2886	1.6577	1.9799	2.3578	2.6174
∞	0.6745	1.2816	1.6449	1.9600	2.3263	2.5758

Critical Values of χ^2

*For a particular number of degrees of freedom,
entry represents the critical value of χ^2
corresponding to a specified upper tail area (α)*

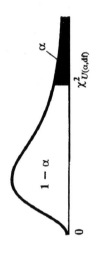

Degrees of Freedom	.995	.99	.975	.95	.90	.75	.25	.10	.05	.025	.01	.005
1			0.001	0.004	0.016	0.102	1.323	2.706	3.841	5.024	6.635	7.879
2	0.010	0.020	0.051	0.103	0.211	0.575	2.773	4.605	5.991	7.378	9.210	10.597
3	0.072	0.115	0.216	0.352	0.584	1.213	4.108	6.251	7.815	9.348	11.345	12.838
4	0.207	0.297	0.484	0.711	1.064	1.923	5.385	7.779	9.488	11.143	13.277	14.860
5	0.412	0.554	0.831	1.145	1.610	2.675	6.626	9.236	11.071	12.833	15.086	16.750
6	0.676	0.872	1.237	1.635	2.204	3.455	7.841	10.645	12.592	14.449	16.812	18.548
7	0.989	1.239	1.690	2.167	2.833	4.255	9.037	12.017	14.067	16.013	18.475	20.278
8	1.344	1.646	2.180	2.733	3.490	5.071	10.219	13.362	15.507	17.535	20.090	21.955
9	1.735	2.088	2.700	3.325	4.168	5.899	11.389	14.684	16.919	19.023	21.666	23.589
10	2.156	2.558	3.247	3.940	4.865	6.737	12.549	15.987	18.307	20.483	23.209	25.188
11	2.603	3.053	3.816	4.575	5.578	7.584	13.701	17.275	19.675	21.920	24.725	26.757
12	3.074	3.571	4.404	5.226	6.304	8.438	14.845	18.549	21.026	23.337	26.217	28.299
13	3.565	4.107	5.009	5.892	7.042	9.299	15.984	19.812	22.362	24.736	27.688	29.819
14	4.075	4.660	5.629	6.571	7.790	10.165	17.117	21.064	23.685	26.119	29.141	31.319
15	4.601	5.229	6.262	7.261	8.547	11.037	18.245	22.307	24.996	27.488	30.578	32.801
16	5.142	5.812	6.908	7.962	9.312	11.912	19.369	23.542	26.296	28.845	32.000	34.267
17	5.697	6.408	7.564	8.672	10.085	12.792	20.489	24.769	27.587	30.191	33.409	35.718
18	6.265	7.015	8.231	9.390	10.865	13.675	21.605	25.989	28.869	31.526	34.805	37.156
19	6.844	7.633	8.907	10.117	11.651	14.562	22.718	27.204	30.144	32.852	36.191	38.582
20	7.434	8.260	9.591	10.851	12.443	15.452	23.828	28.412	31.410	34.170	37.566	39.997
21	8.034	8.897	10.283	11.591	13.240	16.344	24.935	29.615	32.671	35.479	38.932	41.401
22	8.643	9.542	10.982	12.338	14.042	17.240	26.039	30.813	33.924	36.781	40.289	42.796
23	9.260	10.196	11.689	13.091	14.848	18.137	27.141	32.007	35.172	38.076	41.638	44.181
24	9.886	10.856	12.401	13.848	15.659	19.037	28.241	33.196	36.415	39.364	42.980	45.559
25	10.520	11.524	13.120	14.611	16.473	19.939	29.339	34.382	37.652	40.646	44.314	46.928
26	11.160	12.198	13.844	15.379	17.292	20.843	30.435	35.563	38.885	41.923	45.642	48.290
27	11.808	12.879	14.573	16.151	18.114	21.749	31.528	36.741	40.113	43.194	46.963	49.645
28	12.461	13.565	15.308	16.928	18.939	22.657	32.620	37.916	41.337	44.461	48.278	50.993
29	13.121	14.257	16.047	17.708	19.768	23.567	33.711	39.087	42.557	45.722	49.588	52.336
30	13.787	14.954	16.791	18.493	20.599	24.478	34.800	40.256	43.773	46.979	50.892	53.672

Upper Tail Areas (α)

For larger values of degrees of freedom (df) the expression $Z = \sqrt{2x^2} - \sqrt{2(df)} - 1$ may be used and the resulting upper tail area can be obtained from the table of the standardized normal distribution (Table E.2a).

Critical Values of F

For a particular combination of numerator and denominator degrees of freedom, entry represents the critical values of F corresponding to a specified upper tail area (α)

$\alpha = .05$

$F_{U(\alpha,\, df_1, df_2)}$

Denominator d.f.$_2$	Numerator, d.f.$_1$																		
	1	2	3	4	5	6	7	8	9	10	12	15	20	24	30	40	60	120	∞
1	161.4	199.5	215.7	224.6	230.2	234.0	236.8	238.9	240.5	241.9	243.9	245.9	248.0	249.1	250.1	251.1	252.2	253.3	254.3
2	18.51	19.00	19.16	19.25	19.30	19.33	19.35	19.37	19.38	19.40	19.41	19.43	19.45	19.45	19.46	19.47	19.48	19.49	19.50
3	10.13	9.55	9.28	9.12	9.01	8.94	8.89	8.85	8.81	8.79	8.74	8.70	8.66	8.64	8.62	8.59	8.57	8.55	8.53
4	7.71	6.94	6.59	6.39	6.26	6.16	6.09	6.04	6.00	5.96	5.91	5.86	5.80	5.77	5.75	5.72	5.69	5.66	5.63
5	6.61	5.79	5.41	5.19	5.05	4.95	4.88	4.82	4.77	4.74	4.68	4.62	4.56	4.53	4.50	4.46	4.43	4.40	4.36
6	5.99	5.14	4.76	4.53	4.39	4.28	4.21	4.15	4.10	4.06	4.00	3.94	3.87	3.84	3.81	3.77	3.74	3.70	3.67
7	5.59	4.74	4.35	4.12	3.97	3.87	3.79	3.73	3.68	3.64	3.57	3.51	3.44	3.41	3.38	3.34	3.30	3.27	3.23
8	5.32	4.46	4.07	3.84	3.69	3.58	3.50	3.44	3.39	3.35	3.28	3.22	3.15	3.12	3.08	3.04	3.01	2.97	2.93
9	5.12	4.26	3.86	3.63	3.48	3.37	3.29	3.23	3.18	3.14	3.07	3.01	2.94	2.90	2.86	2.83	2.79	2.75	2.71
10	4.96	4.10	3.71	3.48	3.33	3.22	3.14	3.07	3.02	2.98	2.91	2.85	2.77	2.74	2.70	2.66	2.62	2.58	2.54
11	4.84	3.98	3.59	3.36	3.20	3.09	3.01	2.95	2.90	2.85	2.79	2.72	2.65	2.61	2.57	2.53	2.49	2.45	2.40
12	4.75	3.89	3.49	3.26	3.11	3.00	2.91	2.85	2.80	2.75	2.69	2.62	2.54	2.51	2.47	2.43	2.38	2.34	2.30
13	4.67	3.81	3.41	3.18	3.03	2.92	2.83	2.77	2.71	2.67	2.60	2.53	2.46	2.42	2.38	2.34	2.30	2.25	2.21
14	4.60	3.74	3.34	3.11	2.96	2.85	2.76	2.70	2.65	2.60	2.53	2.46	2.39	2.35	2.31	2.27	2.22	2.18	2.13
15	4.54	3.68	3.29	3.06	2.90	2.79	2.71	2.64	2.59	2.54	2.48	2.40	2.33	2.29	2.25	2.20	2.16	2.11	2.07
16	4.49	3.63	3.24	3.01	2.85	2.74	2.66	2.59	2.54	2.49	2.42	2.35	2.28	2.24	2.19	2.15	2.11	2.06	2.01
17	4.45	3.59	3.20	2.96	2.81	2.70	2.61	2.55	2.49	2.45	2.38	2.31	2.23	2.19	2.15	2.10	2.06	2.01	1.96
18	4.41	3.55	3.16	2.93	2.77	2.66	2.58	2.51	2.46	2.41	2.34	2.27	2.19	2.15	2.11	2.06	2.02	1.97	1.92
19	4.38	3.52	3.13	2.90	2.74	2.63	2.54	2.48	2.42	2.38	2.31	2.23	2.16	2.11	2.07	2.03	1.98	1.93	1.88
20	4.35	3.49	3.10	2.87	2.71	2.60	2.51	2.45	2.39	2.35	2.28	2.20	2.12	2.08	2.04	1.99	1.95	1.90	1.84
21	4.32	3.47	3.07	2.84	2.68	2.57	2.49	2.42	2.37	2.32	2.25	2.18	2.10	2.05	2.01	1.96	1.92	1.87	1.81
22	4.30	3.44	3.05	2.82	2.66	2.55	2.46	2.40	2.34	2.30	2.23	2.15	2.07	2.03	1.98	1.94	1.89	1.84	1.78
23	4.28	3.42	3.03	2.80	2.64	2.53	2.44	2.37	2.32	2.27	2.20	2.13	2.05	2.01	1.96	1.91	1.86	1.81	1.76
24	4.26	3.40	3.01	2.78	2.62	2.51	2.42	2.36	2.30	2.25	2.18	2.11	2.03	1.98	1.94	1.89	1.84	1.79	1.73
25	4.24	3.39	2.99	2.76	2.60	2.49	2.40	2.34	2.28	2.24	2.16	2.09	2.01	1.96	1.92	1.87	1.82	1.77	1.71
26	4.23	3.37	2.98	2.74	2.59	2.47	2.39	2.32	2.27	2.22	2.15	2.07	1.99	1.95	1.90	1.85	1.80	1.75	1.69
27	4.21	3.35	2.96	2.73	2.57	2.46	2.37	2.31	2.25	2.20	2.13	2.06	1.97	1.93	1.88	1.84	1.79	1.73	1.67
28	4.20	3.34	2.95	2.71	2.56	2.45	2.36	2.29	2.24	2.19	2.12	2.04	1.96	1.91	1.87	1.82	1.77	1.71	1.65
29	4.18	3.33	2.93	2.70	2.55	2.43	2.35	2.28	2.22	2.18	2.10	2.03	1.94	1.90	1.85	1.81	1.75	1.70	1.64
30	4.17	3.32	2.92	2.69	2.53	2.42	2.33	2.27	2.21	2.16	2.09	2.01	1.93	1.89	1.84	1.79	1.74	1.68	1.62
40	4.08	3.23	2.84	2.61	2.45	2.34	2.25	2.18	2.12	2.08	2.00	1.92	1.84	1.79	1.74	1.69	1.64	1.58	1.51
60	4.00	3.15	2.76	2.53	2.37	2.25	2.17	2.10	2.04	1.99	1.92	1.84	1.75	1.70	1.65	1.59	1.53	1.47	1.39
120	3.92	3.07	2.68	2.45	2.29	2.17	2.09	2.02	1.96	1.91	1.83	1.75	1.66	1.61	1.55	1.50	1.43	1.35	1.25
∞	3.84	3.00	2.60	2.37	2.21	2.10	2.01	1.94	1.88	1.83	1.75	1.67	1.57	1.52	1.46	1.39	1.32	1.22	1.00

continued

Critical Values of F (continued)

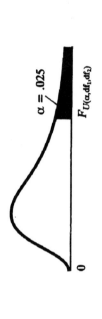

$\alpha = .025$

$F_{U(\alpha, df_1, df_2)}$

Denominator d.f.$_2$	Numerator, d.f.$_1$																		
	1	2	3	4	5	6	7	8	9	10	12	15	20	24	30	40	60	120	∞
1	647.8	799.5	864.2	899.6	921.8	937.1	948.2	956.7	963.3	968.6	976.7	984.9	993.1	997.2	1001	1006	1010	1014	1018
2	38.51	39.00	39.17	39.25	39.30	39.33	39.36	39.37	39.39	39.40	39.41	39.43	39.45	39.46	39.46	39.47	39.48	39.49	39.50
3	17.44	16.04	15.44	15.10	14.88	14.73	14.62	14.54	14.47	14.42	14.34	14.25	14.17	14.12	14.08	14.04	13.99	13.95	13.90
4	12.22	10.65	9.98	9.60	9.36	9.20	9.07	8.98	8.90	8.84	8.75	8.66	8.56	8.51	8.46	8.41	8.36	8.31	8.26
5	10.01	8.43	7.76	7.39	7.15	6.98	6.85	6.76	6.68	6.62	6.52	6.43	6.33	6.28	6.23	6.18	6.12	6.07	6.02
6	8.81	7.26	6.60	6.23	5.99	5.82	5.70	5.60	5.52	5.46	5.37	5.27	5.17	5.12	5.07	5.01	4.96	4.90	4.85
7	8.07	6.54	5.89	5.52	5.29	5.12	4.99	4.90	4.82	4.76	4.67	4.57	4.47	4.42	4.36	4.31	4.25	4.20	4.14
8	7.57	6.06	5.42	5.05	4.82	4.65	4.53	4.43	4.36	4.30	4.20	4.10	4.00	3.95	3.89	3.84	3.78	3.73	3.67
9	7.21	5.71	5.08	4.72	4.48	4.32	4.20	4.10	4.03	3.96	3.87	3.77	3.67	3.61	3.56	3.51	3.45	3.39	3.33
10	6.94	5.46	4.83	4.47	4.24	4.07	3.95	3.85	3.78	3.72	3.62	3.52	3.42	3.37	3.31	3.26	3.20	3.14	3.08
11	6.72	5.26	4.63	4.28	4.04	3.88	3.76	3.66	3.59	3.53	3.43	3.33	3.23	3.17	3.12	3.06	3.00	2.94	2.88
12	6.55	5.10	4.47	4.12	3.89	3.73	3.61	3.51	3.44	3.37	3.28	3.18	3.07	3.02	2.96	2.91	2.86	2.79	2.72
13	6.41	4.97	4.35	4.00	3.77	3.60	3.48	3.39	3.31	3.25	3.15	3.05	2.95	2.89	2.84	2.78	2.72	2.66	2.60
14	6.30	4.86	4.24	3.89	3.66	3.50	3.38	3.29	3.21	3.15	3.05	2.95	2.84	2.79	2.73	2.67	2.61	2.55	2.49
15	6.20	4.77	4.15	3.80	3.58	3.41	3.29	3.20	3.12	3.06	2.96	2.86	2.76	2.70	2.64	2.59	2.52	2.46	2.40
16	6.12	4.69	4.08	3.73	3.50	3.34	3.22	3.12	3.05	2.99	2.89	2.79	2.68	2.63	2.57	2.51	2.45	2.38	2.32
17	6.04	4.62	4.01	3.66	3.44	3.28	3.16	3.06	2.98	2.92	2.82	2.72	2.62	2.56	2.50	2.44	2.38	2.32	2.25
18	5.98	4.56	3.95	3.61	3.38	3.22	3.10	3.01	2.93	2.87	2.77	2.67	2.56	2.50	2.44	2.38	2.32	2.26	2.19
19	5.92	4.51	3.90	3.56	3.33	3.17	3.05	2.96	2.88	2.82	2.72	2.62	2.51	2.45	2.39	2.33	2.27	2.20	2.13
20	5.87	4.46	3.86	3.51	3.29	3.13	3.01	2.91	2.84	2.77	2.68	2.57	2.46	2.41	2.35	2.29	2.22	2.16	2.09
21	5.83	4.42	3.82	3.48	3.25	3.09	2.97	2.87	2.80	2.73	2.64	2.53	2.42	2.37	2.31	2.25	2.18	2.11	2.04
22	5.79	4.38	3.78	3.44	3.22	3.05	2.93	2.84	2.76	2.70	2.60	2.50	2.39	2.33	2.27	2.21	2.14	2.08	2.00
23	5.75	4.35	3.75	3.41	3.18	3.02	2.90	2.81	2.73	2.67	2.57	2.47	2.36	2.30	2.24	2.18	2.11	2.04	1.97
24	5.72	4.32	3.72	3.38	3.15	2.99	2.87	2.78	2.70	2.64	2.54	2.44	2.33	2.27	2.21	2.15	2.08	2.01	1.94
25	5.69	4.29	3.69	3.35	3.13	2.97	2.85	2.75	2.68	2.61	2.51	2.41	2.30	2.24	2.18	2.12	2.05	1.98	1.91
26	5.66	4.27	3.67	3.33	3.10	2.94	2.82	2.73	2.65	2.59	2.49	2.39	2.28	2.22	2.16	2.09	2.03	1.95	1.88
27	5.63	4.24	3.65	3.31	3.08	2.92	2.80	2.71	2.63	2.57	2.47	2.36	2.25	2.19	2.13	2.07	2.00	1.93	1.85
28	5.61	4.22	3.63	3.29	3.06	2.90	2.78	2.69	2.61	2.55	2.45	2.34	2.23	2.17	2.11	2.05	1.98	1.91	1.83
29	5.59	4.20	3.61	3.27	3.04	2.88	2.76	2.67	2.59	2.53	2.43	2.32	2.21	2.15	2.09	2.03	1.96	1.89	1.81
30	5.57	4.18	3.59	3.25	3.03	2.87	2.75	2.65	2.57	2.51	2.41	2.31	2.20	2.14	2.07	2.01	1.94	1.87	1.79
40	5.42	4.05	3.46	3.13	2.90	2.74	2.62	2.53	2.45	2.39	2.29	2.18	2.07	2.01	1.94	1.88	1.80	1.72	1.64
60	5.29	3.93	3.34	3.01	2.79	2.63	2.51	2.41	2.33	2.27	2.17	2.06	1.94	1.88	1.82	1.74	1.67	1.58	1.48
120	5.15	3.80	3.23	2.89	2.67	2.52	2.39	2.30	2.22	2.16	2.05	1.94	1.82	1.76	1.69	1.61	1.53	1.43	1.31
∞	5.02	3.69	3.12	2.79	2.57	2.41	2.29	2.19	2.11	2.05	1.94	1.83	1.71	1.64	1.57	1.48	1.39	1.27	1.00

140

Critical Values of F (continued)

$\alpha = .01$

$F_{U(\alpha, df_1, df_2)}$

Denominator d.f.₂	Numerator, d.f.₁																		
	1	2	3	4	5	6	7	8	9	10	12	15	20	24	30	40	60	120	∞
1	4052	4999.5	5403	5625	5764	5859	5928	5982	6022	6056	6106	6157	6209	6235	6261	6287	6313	6339	6366
2	98.50	99.00	99.17	99.25	99.30	99.33	99.36	99.37	99.39	99.40	99.42	99.43	99.45	99.46	99.47	99.47	99.48	99.49	99.50
3	34.12	30.82	29.46	28.71	28.24	27.91	27.67	27.49	27.35	27.23	27.05	26.87	26.69	26.60	26.50	26.41	26.32	26.22	26.13
4	21.20	18.00	16.69	15.98	15.52	15.21	14.98	14.80	14.66	14.55	14.37	14.20	14.02	13.93	13.84	13.75	13.65	13.56	13.46
5	16.26	13.27	12.06	11.39	10.97	10.67	10.46	10.29	10.16	10.05	9.89	9.72	9.55	9.47	9.38	9.29	9.20	9.11	9.02
6	13.75	10.92	9.78	9.15	8.75	8.47	8.26	8.10	7.98	7.87	7.72	7.56	7.40	7.31	7.23	7.14	7.06	6.97	6.88
7	12.25	9.55	8.45	7.85	7.46	7.19	6.99	6.84	6.72	6.62	6.47	6.31	6.16	6.07	5.99	5.91	5.82	5.74	5.65
8	11.26	8.65	7.59	7.01	6.63	6.37	6.18	6.03	5.91	5.81	5.67	5.52	5.36	5.28	5.20	5.12	5.03	4.95	4.86
9	10.56	8.02	6.99	6.42	6.06	5.80	5.61	5.47	5.35	5.26	5.11	4.96	4.81	4.73	4.65	4.57	4.48	4.40	4.31
10	10.04	7.56	6.55	5.99	5.64	5.39	5.20	5.06	4.94	4.85	4.71	4.56	4.41	4.33	4.25	4.17	4.08	4.00	3.91
11	9.65	7.21	6.22	5.67	5.32	5.07	4.89	4.74	4.63	4.54	4.40	4.25	4.10	4.02	3.94	3.86	3.78	3.69	3.60
12	9.33	6.93	5.95	5.41	5.06	4.82	4.64	4.50	4.39	4.30	4.16	4.01	3.86	3.78	3.70	3.62	3.54	3.45	3.36
13	9.07	6.70	5.74	5.21	4.86	4.62	4.44	4.30	4.19	4.10	3.96	3.82	3.66	3.59	3.51	3.43	3.34	3.25	3.17
14	8.86	6.51	5.56	5.04	4.69	4.46	4.28	4.14	4.03	3.94	3.80	3.66	3.51	3.43	3.35	3.27	3.18	3.09	3.00
15	8.68	6.36	5.42	4.89	4.56	4.32	4.14	4.00	3.89	3.80	3.67	3.52	3.37	3.29	3.21	3.13	3.05	2.96	2.87
16	8.53	6.23	5.29	4.77	4.44	4.20	4.03	3.89	3.78	3.69	3.55	3.41	3.26	3.18	3.10	3.02	2.93	2.84	2.75
17	8.40	6.11	5.18	4.67	4.34	4.10	3.93	3.79	3.68	3.59	3.46	3.31	3.16	3.08	3.00	2.92	2.83	2.75	2.65
18	8.29	6.01	5.09	4.58	4.25	4.01	3.84	3.71	3.60	3.51	3.37	3.23	3.08	3.00	2.92	2.84	2.75	2.66	2.57
19	8.18	5.93	5.01	4.50	4.17	3.94	3.77	3.63	3.52	3.43	3.30	3.15	3.00	2.92	2.84	2.76	2.67	2.58	2.49
20	8.10	5.85	4.94	4.43	4.10	3.87	3.70	3.56	3.46	3.37	3.23	3.09	2.94	2.86	2.78	2.69	2.61	2.52	2.42
21	8.02	5.78	4.87	4.37	4.04	3.81	3.64	3.51	3.40	3.31	3.17	3.03	2.88	2.80	2.72	2.64	2.55	2.46	2.36
22	7.95	5.72	4.82	4.31	3.99	3.76	3.59	3.45	3.35	3.26	3.12	2.98	2.83	2.75	2.67	2.58	2.50	2.40	2.31
23	7.88	5.66	4.76	4.26	3.94	3.71	3.54	3.41	3.30	3.21	3.07	2.93	2.78	2.70	2.62	2.54	2.45	2.35	2.26
24	7.82	5.61	4.72	4.22	3.90	3.67	3.50	3.36	3.26	3.17	3.03	2.89	2.74	2.66	2.58	2.49	2.40	2.31	2.21
25	7.77	5.57	4.68	4.18	3.85	3.63	3.46	3.32	3.22	3.13	2.99	2.85	2.70	2.62	2.54	2.45	2.36	2.27	2.17
26	7.72	5.53	4.64	4.14	3.82	3.59	3.42	3.29	3.18	3.09	2.96	2.81	2.66	2.58	2.50	2.42	2.33	2.23	2.13
27	7.68	5.49	4.60	4.11	3.78	3.56	3.39	3.26	3.15	3.06	2.93	2.78	2.63	2.55	2.47	2.38	2.29	2.20	2.10
28	7.64	5.45	4.57	4.07	3.75	3.53	3.36	3.23	3.12	3.03	2.90	2.75	2.60	2.52	2.44	2.35	2.26	2.17	2.06
29	7.60	5.42	4.54	4.04	3.73	3.50	3.33	3.20	3.09	3.00	2.87	2.73	2.57	2.49	2.41	2.33	2.23	2.14	2.03
30	7.56	5.39	4.51	4.02	3.70	3.47	3.30	3.17	3.07	2.98	2.84	2.70	2.55	2.47	2.39	2.30	2.21	2.11	2.01
40	7.31	5.18	4.31	3.83	3.51	3.29	3.12	2.99	2.89	2.80	2.66	2.52	2.37	2.29	2.20	2.11	2.02	1.92	1.80
60	7.08	4.98	4.13	3.65	3.34	3.12	2.95	2.82	2.72	2.63	2.50	2.35	2.20	2.12	2.03	1.94	1.84	1.73	1.60
120	6.85	4.79	3.95	3.48	3.17	2.96	2.79	2.66	2.56	2.47	2.34	2.19	2.03	1.95	1.88	1.76	1.66	1.53	1.38
∞	6.63	4.61	3.78	3.32	3.02	2.80	2.64	2.51	2.41	2.32	2.18	2.04	1.88	1.79	1.70	1.59	1.47	1.32	1.00

continued

Index

YES!! I would like a copy of the Dissertation Cookbook sent to:

Name _____

Address _____

City _____ State_____ Zip _____

Telephone ( ) _____

Enclosed, please find a check for_____ copies of the Dissertation Cookbook at $39 each for a total of $_____, which includes shipping, handling and any applicable tax. [For first class shipping add $5.00/order]

Make check's payable to:

Best-Prep, LLC
Dissertation Cookbook
15050 Rancho Real
Del Mar, Ca. 92014
Or e-mail: msimon@waldenu.edu

We appreciate your order and are pleased to offer you this service. We would also appreciate your comments about your Dissertation Cookbook.

Did your Dissertation Cookbook meet your expectations? _____Explain: _____

_____
What part(s) did you find the most useful?

How could your Dissertation Cookbook be amended to better suit your needs?I would like a list of other books by Drs. Simon and Francis. (Please fill out the information below if it is different from above address):

Your Name _____ School _____

Mailing Address   _____

                       _____

                       _____